The
Truth
About
Pot

Ten Marijuana Users
Share Their Personal Stories

Joanne Baum, Ph.D.

JOHNSON  INSTITUTE

HAZELDEN®

Hazelden
Center City, Minnesota 55012-0176

1-800-328-9000
1-651-213-4590 (Fax)
www.hazelden.org

Table of Contents

Dedicated to anyone interested in knowing more about chemical dependence and marijuana.

Foreword

Joanne Baum's book could not have come along at a more important time. After years of decline, marijuana use in the United States is increasing at an alarming rate. In 1992, the number of individuals smoking marijuana was up for the first time since 1979. The 1994 National Household Survey on Drug Abuse, compiled by the National Institute on Drug Abuse (NIDA) reported that about 7.3 percent of American teenagers, about 1.3 million adolescents between the ages of 12 and 17 smoked marijuana in 1994. That figure is up 4 percent from NIDA's 1992 survey, and expectations for the 1996 survey are for yet another increase. President Clinton's national drug policy coordinator, Lee Brown, reported that marijuana now accounts for 81 percent of this nation's illicit drug use, and its rise among teenagers reflects a growing sense that marijuana is benign. According to Brown, only 42 percent of teenagers consider marijuana a dangerous drug.

Adolescents don't think of marijuana as dangerous because many of their parents and older role models don't consider marijuana to be a dangerous drug. Even though there is ample evidence that marijuana is a dangerous substance, the extreme claims from both ends of the spectrum have tended to cloud the clinical and human reality of marijuana use.

The truth is that marijuana is a dangerous and debilitating drug. Like those of tobacco, many of its deleterious

1

effects are long-term and long-lasting. The nature of the drug promotes a degree of denial that is both subtle and insidious. Individuals who have chronically used marijuana may be years into abstinence and recovery from their use before they become fully aware of the extent to which their lives have been damaged by that use.

In her book, Dr. Baum graphically presents the human side of marijuana abuse. Through a series of in-depth case studies, based on interviews with individuals who have experienced varying degrees of *cannabis* dependence, she unmasks the subtle and long-lasting effects of marijuana as they manifested themselves in these people's lives. The survivors of marijuana dependence who were interviewed for the book have done a great service for their fellows who may still be using marijuana by candidly describing their experience of how the drug affected all aspects of their lives. Joanne Baum has further clarified marijuana's impact on these individuals through a final chapter that provides her clinical insight in interpreting what they have to say.

In a country where deaths from tobacco use have escalated past 400,000 per year despite major public health prevention efforts, I am appalled by the thought that legalized marijuana would most likely be marketed by the tobacco industry. Conceivably, it would be marketed aggressively to youth in a fashion similar to that which cigarettes are currently marketed. In the face of this potential threat, we need more books like this one by Joanne Baum that present the dispassionate truth about marijuana and its effects.

David E. Smith, M.D.
Founder and Director, Haight Ashbury Free Medical
Clinics

Acknowledgments

I can't thank Leo and Arvilla Berger enough. They thought this was a worthwhile project and believed I could write it. This book would not have been possible without their generous support.

My sincere appreciation and gratitude go to the ten people who made this book possible by sharing their stories. The whole story of marijuana had to be told but I wanted it to be an honest, sincere, personal, and readable story rather than a clinical presentation. Thank you for making this book what I hoped it could be. I have protected people's anonymity by changing names, locations, and professions at times.

I am grateful to the Johnson Institute for recognizing the need for a book like this and for the work and support that was necessary to make it a reality.

My husband has been very supportive, especially during evenings and weekends of writing and editing. His professional experience and understanding have contributed greatly to my clinical work and thus to my writing as well.

My son enjoys having a mother who writes. He often makes his own books, stapling paper together and coloring on the pages. It has been much easier for him to make his books happen than it has been for me. He has been a great model for me.

I also want to thank my parents, who first instilled a love for storytelling by reading and telling me stories when I was little. Ever since then, I've found writing to be a magical process.

Many colleagues and friends have been very supportive of my writing and of this project in particular. I can't name them all here, but I do want to especially thank Dr. Carole Campana, Rick Seymour, and David Smith, who have encouraged me, stood behind me, and cheered me on.

My original desire to write this book came from people who walked into my office saying they were having problems and wondering if smoking marijuana was somehow connected to their problems. There were also people who came in convinced that marijuana didn't have anything to do with their problems but, over time, were willing to see a connection. We learned together. And there were those who came in and refused to see any connection and couldn't let go of their pot. A seed was planted in my head when I saw how hard it was to give up this supposedly benign drug. I thought maybe a book of inspirational stories and little known facts would help. This is the book that grew from that seed.

As I was putting the finishing edits into this manuscript, I received a call from an old friend letting me know that another dear, close friend of mine had just died of a heart attack. He was one of those people who never "got" recovery. He "used" to the end. He taught me how painful this disease can be to people who care about you. Seven years ago he went through a treatment program, believing his alcohol and cocaine consumption to be his only problems. He couldn't hear the professionals telling him that he was chemically dependent and that marijuana was a big part of his addiction. He came out convinced he could still smoke

4

pot and occasionally drink a beer, but no hard stuff. I tried to warn him as did countless others, but he didn't listen. He was determined to live life his way, and he did until he died prematurely. I feel for his children.

Jack M., may you rest in peace.

CHAPTER ONE

A Good, Hard Look at Marijuana

Marijuana is the second most popular drug after alcohol in our country today. So many people smoke marijuana that the numbers alone seem to legitimize and condone its presence in people's lives. Yet, even in moderation marijuana is not "safe." Somehow this information has not filtered down to people who think they are smoking a fairly innocuous drug. Our society perpetuates the myths about pot being a fun, harmless, recreational drug. These myths feed into people's denial of marijuana's problems. To get the entire picture, let's take a good, hard look at pot.

When we look at pot historically since it hit the streets in the sixties through today, there are some interesting trends. First, we had the "groovy" hippies smoking back in the late sixties. They saw pot as a natural, harmless herb that loosened them up so they could discuss and solve the world's problems. It seemed easier to "fight the system" when they were high. Then we had the generation of pot-smoking people in the early seventies whose favorite expression was "far-out." They were still somewhat political, but not at all as committed to action as many of the hippies had been. Pot smoking was then passed down to the "rad" and "awesome" generation of the eighties, where most vestiges of smoking, philosophizing, planning, or taking action had long since gone by the wayside. They just liked being high for the sake of being high. And today, we have children of former hippies or "far-out" seventies smokers who are now the "Hey, dude" pot smokers of the nineties. They mostly want to change how they are feeling, have fun, and party. What users today don't realize is that the marijuana available today is not as benign a drug as it was back in the sixties. Today's "high" is different from the "high" people were getting thirty years ago.

Yet the myths continue. If people attribute any side effects to pot, it's usually "the munchies." People find their increased eating to be annoying if they're weight-conscious, or fun if they're not. Many people who smoke pot regularly see themselves as law-abiding citizens, certainly not criminals; they just "ignore" the law in this one instance. Most people who smoke marijuana thinks it's worth any minimal risk they may perceive. They hold down jobs. They function, so they think, "What's the big deal?"

One aspect of the "big deal" is that people really do get addicted to pot, just as they get addicted to alcohol, cocaine, heroin, valium, or any other mind-altering chemical. Another important but disregarded aspect is, that as marijuana has gotten stronger, so have its side effects. It affects all the organs in your body. For instance, it's worse on your lungs and respiratory system than cigarettes. It affects your emotions, your moods, your drive, your productivity, your attitudes, and your thinking. Most pot smokers say it's worth it. But is it?

Pot's Insidious Side Effects

Besides society's ignorance and myths that pot is a "safe" drug, there are other reasons why it is difficult to detect and do anything about a problem with this particular drug. I label them "pot's insidious side effects." These include: (A) lethargy; (B) poor concentration; (C) lack of motivation; (D) depression; (E) paranoia; (F) isolation; and (G) physiological effects. Taking these seven side effects into account, it's understandable why people have a more difficult time trying to stay away from pot than other more obviously debilitating drugs.

Have you known people who never stopped smoking marijuana and have not quite lived up to their true potential? Do you know people whose emotions never fully developed because whenever they've been faced with emotional situations, they've always gotten high? They probably see pot as something they can count on, something that helps smooth the edges, kind of like a best friend. They haven't developed other strategies because marijuana is always available. They don't realize that the more they smoke marijuana in response to emotional or complex situations, the more they'll need to smoke it simply because they don't know how else to handle themselves or their emotions.

Sometimes people get fleeting glimpses that smoking pot may not be such a great solution, but they don't know what to do with their suspicions. They don't want them to be true because they don't know how else to handle things. Their emotions were stunted when they started smoking marijuana regularly, but they don't know it because marijuana distorts their thinking. They want to believe they're handling everything well enough most of the time. They probably have occasional internal debates going on: "Could it be the pot?" "Nah, it's only pot." "But why is life getting painful, confusing, irritating, unclear, depressing, and even scary?"

Pot is relatively inexpensive. Pot smokers probably won't have to foreclose on their house because they've been buying pot regularly. But they could end up in foreclosure if they become unable to concentrate and produce at work and lose their jobs as a consequence of chronic pot use. They might then have trouble finding another job because they just can't get motivated to look for one. They may start running out of extra funds, missing a mortgage payment or two, but don't feel bothered by it too much. After all, they could escape with a little pot.

That scenario can happen so gradually that it would be relatively easy to blame other things. People in those circumstances still view pot as the one thing that's helping them get through the crises happening around them. After all, it makes them feel better, it calms them down, it makes things easier to take. But, over time, when reality doesn't match what they'd like it to be and the common denominator is pot, there's probably a drug problem being ignored.

A woman I once spoke to was convinced she was a safe driver when she was stoned:

When I was smoking pot every day, I was convinced I was a better driver stoned than straight. Convinced! Nobody could dispute my perception (which I took as fact) that I was more alert, attentive, and responsive when I was high. Yet now, after doing some reading about marijuana, I know my opinions had been based on an altered reality (produced by the pot), which allowed me to believe my own inaccurate perceptions. The research I read concluded that marijuana doesn't make you more perceptive. It makes you less perceptive. It also slows down your physical and cognitive response time. I used to be so sure my responses were even more keen when I was high than when I wasn't, but I was just fooling myself. Reality and my perceptions didn't match. It's a miracle I never got into any accidents given how many times I got into the drivers' seat of my car, lit up a joint, and drove."

Marijuana Dependence

Many people can smoke pot without becoming addicted; we know that. It's also true that many people can drink alcohol and not suffer any alcoholic consequences. So does that mean alcohol is benign? We know it's not for many people. But pot can creep up on you; the consequences can be insidious, difficult to see, and easy to deny or ignore. Oliwenstein (1988)* reports that around 10 percent of marijuana users cannot control their use of the drug. Interestingly, 20 percent of people who drink alcohol cannot control their usage; these people are alcoholics. This 20 percent figure holds true for cocaine users as well. Thus, 20 percent of cocaine users are cocaine addicts. With more accurate information and statistics, will the 10 percent figure Oliwenstein found in 1988 increase?

A number of years ago, I was on a radio talk show in San Francisco. I had been a guest on this show before and the topic had always been cocaine. On this particular night I suggested we talk about pot. "Oh, come on," the host said, "It'll be a dead show." I said, "Maybe, but I don't think so." With some trepidation, we began the hour.

I talked about marijuana being much stronger than it used to be and about people suffering consequences after smoking marijuana for years that they were not attributing to their pot use. I talked about people I had worked with who came in after they began to have gnawing suspicions that something wasn't going right in their life. Often a spouse or partner had suggested they cut down, or grow up, or "do something," but they hadn't linked those complaints or sug-

*Complete references are listed in the appendix.

gestions to smoking pot. After all, most of them were holding down a job, even though it often wasn't quite where they had pictured themselves working ten years before. "Okay, so they needed to make lists and hoped they wouldn't lose their lists so they could perform responsibly, but didn't everyone need lists? Wasn't everyone forgetful? Wasn't everyone irritable and uptight until they could have just a few hits from a joint at night?"

That's basically the way I started the show. The lines started ringing like crazy. As one caller said, "That's me you're talking about. My wife seems to be getting more and more annoyed with me. She says I seem to have lost a lot of my energy. I like to come home from work, get high, and relax. But my day is over before I light up. I hardly ever make exceptions and smoke during the day unless something really stressful has happened. But by evening, I've functioned on the job all day. Why can't I just veg out? She says I'm boring."

He wanted to know if what he and his wife were experiencing could be from the pot. When I suggested he try life without it for awhile and see, he balked. He didn't like the idea at all. I suggested his strong response—not even wanting to try life without pot—indicated how important it was to him. After all, I wasn't saying he should stop for good. I was saying, if you're curious about whether or not "it" could be from the pot, stop smoking for awhile and see what happens. I asked him to look at what his resistance to the idea of a break from pot might mean.

A little later in the conversation he said he was a little worried because his wife seemed to be getting more and more disgusted with him, and he didn't want to lose his marriage just because he liked to "relax." He said, "I'd do anything to save my marriage. I don't want her to go away."

11

I responded by saying, "If you love your wife and would, in your own words, 'Do anything for her,' except take a break from pot, the very thing that might be causing the problems between you two, what does that say to you?" "Oh," he responded, with a dead silence following. "I think I'll have to look at this." Our conversation ended soon after that.

Struggles with Recovery

People I've worked with talk about occasionally feeling high again months after they've stopped smoking. This is fairly common during the first year of sobriety. The reason they feel high again is because their fatty tissues have released stored up pot into their system.

When people withdraw and stop using most other drugs, they feel significantly better within days, weeks, or in the case of valium, at least months after stopping. But with pot it's different. I have often found that marijuana addicts don't feel those, "Aha! My body is feeling different. This is great!" sensations for at least one year. And they don't become clear-headed for up to four years, as you'll see in the stories that follow this chapter.

Because they don't feel significantly different, and because they experience lethargy, a lack of follow-through, and poor concentration, people who come in for help often drop out of treatment. Their impatience takes over. They say they can't see why it's worth it to stay clean and sober, since they don't see or feel very different from when they were smoking. They've developed a "Why bother?" attitude. I try to talk them into holding out longer. I remind them that what they are experiencing as a lackluster view of life is truly a side effect of pot. It's not documented in the research literature, but drug therapists see it all the time.

These side effects also make it easier for a person to ignore the reality that pot is the problem. In order to justify leaving treatment, they'll often point a finger at everyone and everything else around them, blaming them for their problems and minimizing the pot. After all, they quit smoking and, life wasn't much better. The recovery expression, "For every finger pointing at someone else there are at least three pointing back at you," helps people see this differently. And when they do, they can take responsibility for themselves, their disease, and their recovery. But people who are still in denial looking for an excuse to quit treatment don't see it that way. Unfortunately, the cumulative side effects of chronic pot smoking make it very easy for a person to leave recovery and continue to use.

Research

One woman told me about her decision to begin smoking pot in 1968 when she was fifteen:

> Boy, was my research faulty. My mother was the only one who warned me. She used to say, "The facts aren't all in yet. There's probably more to this drug. What if they find it is indeed dangerous down the line and you'll have been smoking it all along." I don't like the idea of you smoking pot. It could affect your brain cells, your lungs, who knows? Please, honey, you could be doing irreparable harm." But did I listen? Not at all. I wish I had.

Although much research has been done during the past thirty years, there are difficulties in using research results in treatment. The results of one study cannot be compared to the results of another study, because the marijuana used in various studies is not "controlled." THC (the known psy-

13

choactive substance in marijuana) levels, as well as all the other components in marijuana, vary from study to study. They have also varied widely over time as domestic marijuana production has increased.

Since the late seventies, domestic growers have increased the potency of marijuana. As of 1989 the domestically grown pot was 200 times as strong as what had been arriving from Mexico and South America on a regular basis. It's continued to get stronger since then. Thus, more modern studies cannot be compared to earlier studies because the drug itself has changed so much over time.

There are other confounding variables: (A) how much smoke people take into their lungs with each inhalation varies and isn't measurable; (B) how long smokers keep the smoke in their lungs varies from person to person and from study to study; and (C) how much smoke they blow out also varies from person to person and among different studies.

Studies are beginning to bring in evidence strongly suggesting marijuana is a unique psychoactive agent because it has paradoxical effects. It acts as both a stimulant and a depressant at low doses, but mostly as a depressant in higher doses. Marijuana directly affects the central nervous system. It also may affect the immune system, the reproductive system, the respiratory system, and the cardiovascular system. The picture is further compounded because marijuana is not a single drug but a mix of over 60 *cannabinoid* compounds, which makes measuring active levels of all marijuana's elements impossible at this time. Scientists have only been able to study 14 of the 60-odd *cannabinoids* in detail. We have no idea how the other 46 affect the human body (Gold, 1989).

Since most research findings only yield strong possibilities, not indisputable results, a chronic user can easily turn to a drug therapist and say, "See, they don't know for sure. Why stop until they do know? I could be stopping for nothing. Besides, I feel fine now." I try to counter such arguments with, "If life is so good, why are you in my office? Let's deal with your reality and see if it's such a pretty picture. If you want life to be different, then we have something we can work with.

Despite these problems researchers do agree on some results: Marijuana smoke is more dangerous in terms of lung cancer and other respiratory ailments than cigarette smoke; that is a conclusive finding. Marijuana clearly has been linked to short-term memory loss, which seems to be reversible within a few weeks of smoking marijuana for the last time. Marijuana also has been documented to produce certain hormonal changes, which may have serious implications for adolescents. Marijuana seems to affect certain brain chemistry, which may affect the developing adolescent's emotions, but again, we don't know how much or how long. People often experience prolonged depressions after chronic marijuana use.

According to Mark Gold (1989) a typical joint (or cigarette) of marijuana was 1 percent THC by weight or 10 mg of THC in the early 1970s. In 1989 a high-quality joint could easily have 150 mg of THC and double that if it was dipped in hash oil. A user in 1989 could easily be exposed to doses as high as 300 mg from a single joint. Gold's (1989) findings suggest that smoking a daily dose of 180 mg of THC a day for 11–21 days produces a defined withdrawal syndrome. Since 1989 domestic marijuana growers have continued to use sophisticated cultivation techniques, resulting in still stronger strains of marijuana. And a new type of marijuana is being laced with formaldehyde. When you think about potential problems with marijuana, you also have to take into account what adulterants have been added that can cause such serious side effects as acute psychosis and physical toxicity.

Siegel, Garnier, Lindley, and Siegel (1988) found that some of the psycho/physiological problems resulting from pot may be due to mercury inhaled with pot smoke. The mercury comes from soil in parts of Hawaii, California, and Mexico where pot is grown. Plants are particularly likely to pick up mercury from soil near natural volcanic and geothermal sites. When a person smokes and inhales anything grown in mercury rich soil, the lungs absorb 85 percent of the inhaled mercury vapor, which is then distributed to the brain and other organs through the bloodstream (McCarthy, 1989). Some of the problems associated with marijuana such as memory loss, insomnia, lack of self-control, anxiety, irritability, drowsiness, tremors, paranoia, and depression may be partially attributable to an accumulation of mercury from inhaling pot that was grown in mercuriferous soils. It has been impossible to separate the two factors (pot and mercury) to see which is causing what.

In addition, daily marijuana use has been associated with a doubling of the risk for psychosis. The most common type was a brief acute organic reaction characterized by mental dulling, distortion of time, dreamlike euphoria progressing to fragmenting thoughts, and hallucinations. More potent marijuana can cause even more severe reactions.

Cohn (1986) reported that marijuana affects ovulation and sperm production: "If users are not fully matured, their sexual development can be interrupted or even halted." Today's youth may be inadvertently signing on as guinea pigs when they think they're just having fun and getting high. Dr. Virchel Wood of Loma Linda University has observed an increasing number of hand and foot birth defects in babies born to people who have used marijuana. He explains this phenomenon by saying that, since marijuana's chemicals build up particularly in the sex organs where the cells (chromosomes) for producing other human beings are housed, that build-up may cause birth defects. In one study, scientists blew marijuana smoke into the cages of mice for three minutes a day during a ten-day period. That really wasn't very much, even for mice, but when those mice had babies, one out of five offspring had birth defects. They also administered marijuana to female mice. Later the scientists examined the mice's ovaries and found 75 percent of their egg cells were dead or damaged. The scientists were surprised, because female mice seldom have that problem. They concluded that the results were due to marijuana.

Dewey (1986) reported subjective psychological effects of marijuana that included excitement, dissociation of ideas, enhancement of the senses, distortions of time and space, delusional thinking, impulsiveness, illusions, and hallucinations. Dewey (1986), Oliwenstein (1988), and Gold (1989) also reported these psychological effects were often accompanied by objective behavioral changes including a deterioration of psychomotor performance, diminished attention span and memory, as well as reduced physical strength. Studies have shown that motor skills in general (including those needed for safe driving) are impaired for hours or even days after using marijuana. A study by Yesavage, Leirer, Ditman, and Holister (1985) found that pilots displayed significant impairment in their ability to fly as long as 24 hours after smoking marijuana, and they were completely unaware of their poor performance.

Murray (1986), Steele (1989), Porterfield (1989), Gallagher (1988), and Hymes (1989) all found that marijuana affects a person's cognitive functioning. Specific impairments include confusion, loss of directedness, loss of the ability to remember information, and an inability to manipulate thoughts in order to achieve a specific goal. Marijuana users have long reported an enhanced sensory awareness (e.g. visual and auditory acuity), yet the research does not confirm these self-reports. People are experiencing a perceived difference, rather than a real one, such as the pilots who thought they were flying just fine, but if they hadn't been in simulators, they probably would have crashed their planes. Reality and perceptions do not match when a person is smoking marijuana. Flynn and Kaye (1988) add credibility to the "impaired motor skills" findings by reporting that the engineer and brakeman responsible for the 1987 Amtrak disaster near Baltimore, in which 174 people were injured and 15 people died, had been smoking marijuana on the job.

People are unaware of the negative effects that being "high" has on their psychomotor activities. Many accidents may be caused by marijuana-impaired drivers, but since people aren't tested for pot, we just don't know the extent of such incidents. A "momentary lapse of concentration" that caused an accident may be blamed on other sources. I wonder how many of those accidents are actually drug (pot) related. People should not drive a vehicle when they are high or within 24 to 36 hours after smoking marijuana.

Gallagher (1988) reports that young people, pregnant women, nursing mothers, heart patients (because pot can increase a person's heart rate by as much as 90 beats per minute), and emotionally unstable people are most at risk for serious complications from smoking pot. She goes on to report a finding from Dr. Robert Millman of the New York Hospital-Payne Whitney Clinic, which suggests that marijuana can produce a fear of losing control that has induced paranoia and anxiety in marijuana users who have no history of these problems. Miller, Eriksen, and Owley (1994) concur. Dr. Millman also reports that marijuana can trigger latent psychiatric disorders.

In a 1989 *Current Health 2* publication, Kay M. Porterfield reports that marijuana lowered alertness and retarded learning and memory. She suggested that there could be a long-term memory loss. Porterfield (1989) documented a decline in motivation leading to poor grades, low self-esteem, and a loss of career goals among high school students who smoked marijuana.

Adolescents or younger children whose developmental process is not yet complete should not be using at all, yet they're the most likely age group to be experimenting with pot. In October, 1995, *The Weekly Reader* reported the results of a recent study they had conducted with fourth through sixth graders: 26 percent of the students polled said they had friends who were using pot on a weekly basis.

According to a Metropolitan Insurance Company Statistical Bulletin in 1984, more than 50 percent of all marijuana users said they started using pot between the sixth and ninth grades. Gold (1989) was alarmed because people are smoking pot at younger and younger ages, and they're using stronger and stronger pot. We just don't know how the current strong strains will affect them now or in the future, because there aren't any longitudinal studies with today's more potent blends of marijuana. Indications seem to point to possibilities, especially for young people, that pot does affect their physical, hormonal, and emotional development, but we just don't know for sure. In this case, not knowing "reality" is pretty scary, especially for drug counselors who see people experiencing problems not yet documented in the literature. How do they gain people's trust so they believe there are side effects, which may have long-term consequences? It's a difficult job, especially taking into account people's paranoia and cognitive impairment as they're withdrawing from pot.

Telling the Stories

This book presents ten personal stories of individuals who have smoked marijuana, enjoyed it at first, and then found that life with pot wasn't really that much fun after all. They entered recovery in various ways and learned to live life as recovering marijuana addicts. The stories are told in the people's own words with little or no editing, so you can get the feel for each person and what he or she experienced. Their names have been changed to protect their anonymity.

Every person I've ever worked with who comes in wondering about a marijuana problem started smoking pot with the intention of having fun, relaxing, and enjoying one of life's pleasures. They never started out with the goal of becoming an addict. The people interviewed for this book come from different backgrounds, are different ages, and live in very different circumstances. Their common links are their former use of marijuana and the desire to stay clean and sober one day at a time.

The stories are presented in order from the person with the shortest time clean and sober (nine months) to the person with the longest length of sobriety (almost fifteen years). This was done so you can see how people change and discover things about the drug and about their life over time. It really does take a long time for a person to "clear," as one person says in his story. I also purposely chose people from different classes, ages, and professions, for their own unique contributions. These individuals share what life was like before they smoked marijuana, what it was like when they smoked, what got them into recovery, and what life is like now without marijuana. This format of "sharing your experience, strength, and hope" is often used at Twelve Step meetings.

It has been said, "addiction is the only disease where people try like hell *not* to get better." But it *can* be done. It *has* been done one day at a time. There's even a Twelve Step program modeled after Alcoholics Anonymous (A.A.) called Marijuana Anonymous (M.A.). As the people in this book can attest, life can be different than it was. People can recover from pot addiction when they do what it takes to stay clean and sober. (For more information on M.A., see the Appendix.)

An A.A. saying is, "If you go to meetings and don't drink in between, you won't get drunk." Paraphrasing this simple philosophy, "If you go to meetings and don't smoke pot in between, you won't get high." When people don't get high, their reality begins to match the reality of the world around them and life gets easier, but they have to learn new ways of coping with emotional situations just as the people in this book did.

This book is about recovering from marijuana addiction. You'll see references in each person's story to A.A. and other Twelve Step programs. Recovery is a way of life. It provides you with a new set of tools to deal with life's ups and downs. The reason people say they're "grateful" addicts or alcoholics is that they've been handed a new way of life with an effective set of tools, which they didn't have before. They get to feel better. They have a caring support group at their meetings. They may never have experienced such support before; especially if they grew up in homes where love and support was conditional, unpredictable, and often not forthcoming. The acceptance and support they get in meetings can be very healing in and of itself.

The number of meetings people go to varies widely. Sometimes when people feel "slippery" (like they might use) they'll go to as many as one or two meetings a day. Other people who have incorporated the program into their lives may only go to one meeting a week or one every other week. It varies from person to person and within different situations.

In my role as a chemical dependency therapist, I usually recommend that people attend four or more meetings a week at first and then reduce the number over time as they feel comfortable. I also recommend that people get a sponsor, another person with longer sobriety in the program who helps them with the Steps and is generally there as a sounding board. It's not the number of meetings that influences the quality of sobriety or the effectiveness of an individual recovery program, it's how that person incorporates the information learned at meetings into his or her life.

With this additional information, let's look at people's stories. Then we'll summarize what we've learned about marijuana use and draw some conclusions in the final chapter.

CHAPTER TWO

Debbie

Age 22
Office Worker
Nine Months of Sobriety

I lived in a small town in Pennsylvania until I was about fifteen or sixteen. I have two older half sisters—Jeanne is ten years older than me and Robin is thirteen years older. I have an older brother, Vic, who's four years older than me, and a younger sister named Erin, who's eighteen months younger than me.

There were a lot of times it didn't feel safe in my house. I think my earliest clear memory is from when I was four or five years old. It was also when I knew something was definitely wrong in our family. I walked into the living room one day and saw my dad sitting in a chair staring at a wall, and he stayed there all day! I asked my mom about it, but she didn't respond. I had a lot of psychological stuff left over from that incident: I felt left out, abandoned, rejected. I thought, "What's wrong with me that I can't know what's going on or at least understand it?"

Home was insane—a lot of verbal and physical fighting. I was never physically abused, but my mom, Jeanne, Vic, and Erin were, and I witnessed it. My mom said I was my father's favorite. I guess when Vic was born, Dad had wanted a girl, so he was disappointed. When I was born, he was all excited. When Erin was born, he had already had his little girl....

I went into hiding a lot. I was into my early addictions—books, food, and isolation. I was cute and sweet when I was "out," and then I'd retreat. Sometimes I tried to get in the middle and be peacekeeper. I took on the role of being my mom's protector when I could, but I stayed clear if the fighting was between the two men. That was too scary—time for retreat then...

I witnessed violent scenes between my mom and dad, and it was very upsetting to me. I talked a little to my mom, and we comforted each other during the rages; Erin too. I can remember the three of us huddled together. Oh, and we had a babysitter. I think I talked to her some, but other than that, not much to anyone else.

As we got older, my mother got more and more involved in the peace movement. She made lots of trips to South America. We got to go on marches with her; it was way cool for us, but oh, my God, did it ever cause conflict with my father! She was a housewife at the time. It was kind of neat to have Mom around.

Right before they divorced, there was this one scene where the cops came and took my Dad away. I think one of the kids ran to a neighbor's house where the dad was a cop. My dad was being threatening, violent, and all kinds of nasty stuff.

When I was ten years old, I got kissed by my grandfather.

He came into my room, shut the door, and said, "You're a big girl now," and he made out with me. He asked me how I liked it. I was so scared and so in shock I kind of muttered something. He was a sick man! Later, I got him to come into this tree fort of mine, and you know what I said?, I said,

"Grandpa, I'm your granddaughter, not your girlfriend!" He said, "Okay, okay!" and backed off.

I talked to my mom about it, and she talked to my father about it, but as it turned out, they thought it was my fault. Ha! I knew it was my father and grandmother protecting my grandfather. I was told I ran around with my clothes off, or I had bounced on his lap too much, and he was teaching me a lesson. I was really screwed up about it; you know, "What's reality here?" I think my mom tried to defend me, but she let it go—she was into her fear and her submission. I maintained my stance, and I was in fury!

We moved out shortly after that, when I was eleven. We went and stayed in a women's shelter, because my father wouldn't move out of the house. I think the thing with my grandfather might have been the last straw for my mom. My brother Vic was staying with a friend's family by then. He had been doing that on and off, mostly on for a few years already. It wasn't an official foster family; they just kind of took him in.

When I was living at the shelter, I visited my father once and talked to my grandmother [about the sexual abuse] on the phone. She tried to tell me again that my grandfather was teaching me a lesson, and I think I just screamed into the phone, I mean I completely lost it with my grandmother! I stormed out of the house and ran to a neighbor's. I think my mother eventually picked me up from there. It was definitely a scene. I had a lot of anger and rage at my dad. Around the same time, my mom told us that Dad was on all these drugs, that he'd been smoking pot for years and more recently had gotten into coke. My dad had a workroom that he always locked, and I guess he'd go lock himself in there, so I had never seen him get high. Mom also told us that he had tried to smother her at night, and about other things he had tried to do to her. I went into a state of shock. This was my dad she was talking about. I turned into a basket case. I remember being up in this tree and crying and crying, and I wouldn't come down.

We went from the shelter to my oldest half sister's for about a month or two, and then to our own place about seven miles away from my hometown for a year. My father finally moved out of our house the next year. The house was disgustingly filthy. He must have never done any cleaning. We had to clean it, and clean it, and clean it.

During this whole time my dad said he wouldn't see me unless I went to see my grandparents. I had disowned them, but I gave in and went to see them with my dad when we were still in the shelter. For a long time after that, when I'd be with my dad, I felt disgusted with him. He'd go to kiss me on the cheek, and I'd be like, "Ugh!" That started abating when I was fifteen, sixteen.

When I was twelve, I was seeing a nineteen-year-old guy who turned me on to marijuana. I remember the first joint: I just sucked it in, man, right into my lungs, and *I loved it!* I fell in love. It took me away, made me silly, no worries. I thought, "Life is great, I'm high!" We continued to smoke until I broke up with him, deciding he was too old for me. After that, I made friends with people who did drugs— smoking pot, drinking, and dropping acid. I was twelve the first time I got drunk. I've had bouts with crank [speed] and coke, also, but marijuana's always been my drug of choice.

One day, when I was twelve, I came home with a green mohawk haircut. My mom told me to go to my room. I said, "I'm going out with my friends." She said, "Go to your room. If you go out with your friends, don't bother to come back." So I went to a friend's house and stayed there about a week. The day before my thirteenth birthday she called, asking me to come home for a birthday dinner. I went. She accepted my being a punk rocker, and I moved back home.

I used to get drunk and high with my punk rock friends. Very soon after that I met my best friend, Fay. I was this punk rocker—we're talking leather jacket, combat boots, a green mohawk—and Fay was like this heavy metaller, wearing slutty outfits, long hair, and lots of make-up. We were a pair!

I was miserable as hell during that time! After a group of friends made it clear they had an "Anti-Debbie Association" going, I was crushed. I tried to OD on a bottle of aspirin. I slept for a long time. When I finally woke up, my mother was really angry at me. I remember thinking, "I just tried to kill myself and my mom is yelling at me? Jesus Christ, what's wrong with this picture?"

The only thing that saved me during that time was my friend, Fay. We smoked tons of pot together, listened to music, took walks, and held hands. (We weren't gay or anything, just incredible friends.) A lot of what I turned to was the acceptance of her friendship and, of course, drugs.

My mom met Steve on one of her trips. They started a long-distance relationship. She was really in love. When I was fifteen, she decided to leave Pennsylvania and move to another part of the country to be with him. She gave me the option of leaving or staying. I stayed by myself. Get this: it wasn't quite by myself because, since the divorce, we had boarders in our house. I don't know how responsible it was of my mom, but I stayed in the house with the boarders. I was kind of like landlord, mother, friend—being fifteen, sixteen, on drugs, and working. I had my mom's car for getting around. Some friends of mine moved in, too. People didn't get along too well, so there was still fighting at home.

I can't remember, was I in school during that time? Let's see, I just couldn't make it in regular school in seventh grade. I went to an alternative school. I know I went to eighth and ninth grade, and half of tenth grade. In the middle of tenth grade, I decided I didn't like school—the cliques, the social thing. My mother had home-schooled my younger sister and me for awhile, so I knew that was available. I home-schooled myself through half of tenth grade, eleventh, and twelfth grades. It cost $250 a year, and I paid for it myself. Sometimes I slacked off on my work, but usually I really did it, and I graduated from that school.

We were doing coke one night and had picked up a girl from the neighborhood. She told another friend, that friend told her father who was a cop, and all of a sudden it was like, "What are you doing here? You're a minor; you can't stay here alone." So the boarders stayed, and I moved in with my dad for a month or two, then went to live with my mom and Steve. I worked a few jobs, never lasting very long, did a lot of dope, some acid and coke, went out with a dealer for a year, went with a married man—it was a mess.

Then I visited my sister Jeanne in Colorado. When I got there, I couldn't get hold of any drugs, and I was freaking out! I decided to get clean. I didn't get high for the whole two weeks. I was like, "This is it. This is my solution; I love it here; I'm never going back" (except to pack up my stuff and move). I was eighteen, almost nineteen. When I left, my sister gave me a number to call, and I got the address of an Narcotics Anonymous (N.A.) meeting near where my mom lived. I went to that meeting before I went back to my mother's house. It was a great meeting! I stayed clean the week I was at my mom's packing up. My sister got me a job and an apartment in Colorado, so when I got back, I was set. I went to one more N.A. meeting, but someone gave me something to read, and it was a turn-off. I used it as an excuse to not go back. I got drunk a few times, but stayed clean from pot on my own for four months.

Then I met Bob, my ex-husband. He wasn't an addict or a cigarette smoker, but he used with me occasionally. Isn't that horrible? I coerced him. He moved in with me and for the next two-and-a-half years we were together, we'd break up, then get back together. We had apartments, then we'd lose them. We couldn't pay rent because we were buying dope, and we were both so dysfunctional in the job area. We'd move in with his parents, then back out. We definitely had our ups and downs. He was very nice, except a couple of times he freaked out and did things that were not so cool, like once during an argument, I found myself pinned face down on the bed. Man, was I scared!

I got married mainly because I wanted to be in an intimate relationship and grow and be healthy and settle down and have a family. And I wanted to be taken care of, especially financially. I was all messed up in the job scene. Bob was not very functional either in the work area, so we were always borrowing money. Don't you think it's interesting that I picked a guy to take care of me who wasn't even capable of taking care of himself? I tell you something, I think it's a God thing—it drew me sooner to that place where I needed to take care of myself and get responsible. I'm only 22 now; it could have been worse.

During the marriage I'd smoke all day, although there were a few times when I knew deep down I had a problem and tried to stay clean, like when I went five days without smoking pot. The first time I got high after that, I really freaked out. I didn't want to get high again, yet I forced myself back into active addiction. I *forced* myself back. I was uncomfortable about it as all hell, but I did it anyway, trying to get comfortable again. I got more and more into smoking pot and more hopeless around it, not even trying to stop, saying, "I'm not interested in anything but getting high." If I was out [of pot], I'd freak out until I got some.

In October, 1992, I woke up one morning and said, "I'm gone; I'm leaving." And I went to live with Jeanne for awhile. Then I went back to the Midwest to my mom's for a month. I talked to Bob by phone a few times, and he finally convinced me to come back, saying he had made all this money and gotten us an apartment. It was great for a couple of weeks before I found out he had borrowed the money, and I had come back under all these false pretenses. I felt totally betrayed. There was a violent scene in the car. I packed to leave again, but I went back pretty fast because I didn't want to look bad. I had just moved back to be with him: What would my mother think? And I wanted to be taken care of. I wanted to be happy and married. Things got better. I smoked less and worked more for awhile, but then I got into smoking every day, all day.

When my sister Erin came to visit, it was very easy for me to quit my job. The absurd part is, I don't even know if I saw my sister because we were constantly high. From there I went downhill really fast, smoked all the time, ate all the time—way into food addiction, way into pot addiction. We were borrowing and getting behind in our bills and our rent.

Right around that time (June, 1993) Jeanne got in really bad shape. She had been in recovery for a few months, but had a major depression that ended in a relapse where she was incoherent and suicidal. She called and I went to be with her. That first night she was drunk, and I got high. Throughout the weekend I talked to my mom and Erin back in the Midwest. They kept saying, "Get her to her therapist!" We finally did on Monday, and from there she went into a hospital for a few days, and then into a treatment center. I was supposed to take over her business. I stayed there, got high, and did her business as best I could.

My mother came out for a week or two and stayed at the treatment center. She learned a lot about the disease of addiction. She came home a couple of days before my sister, and I think I was bottoming out in my own way. I think I was ready and just waiting for someone to say something to me. My mom sat me down and said, "You have a disease, you're an addict, you need help. You have a disease, it's like cancer, you can't control it, you need help."

I thought about it the rest of that day, got high that night and the next day, all the while thinking about it. A friend had just given me shitloads of marijuana. I decided it would be my last day getting high. I went to my dealer's house that night and got rid of all my drugs and paraphernalia. The next morning I went and picked up my sister from the treatment center. It was my first day clean.

As soon as Jeanne was in the car, I told her I was trying to clean up, and that I was freaking out. That night Bob took me to a meeting, and I walked in and basically said, "This is my first day clean and I'm scared!" It was so wonderful! They gave me a basic text, *gave* me. I walked out of there with hope. The next few days I was a fucking mess, detoxing and scared to be giving up a friend. I kept talking to myself: "How am I going to survive?" In the past I'd think about the program and say, "Someday I'm going to go back to a meeting, and I'll get clean." I knew I would someday...

I did 90 [meetings] in 90 [days] except for when I got sick. I got into recovery. Bob and I separated. I got involved with another guy in recovery. Bob and I filed for divorce together. I think getting involved with somebody else was my way to get out from Bob and an escape. By two months clean, I was moving in with this guy I had met at one of my first meetings. He had been in the program about a month longer than me. I was waking up as I lived with him and realizing this wasn't what I wanted. I left (after about two months), stayed with a friend, and then moved into this place about five months ago. I love it. I would not give up this apartment unless something miraculous happened. It's my own space; I'm responsible for it, for paying my bills, my rent, and being at work—and I'm doing it! I can go out, I can have people over, I can come home to it.

Yesterday I had nine months in the program. In talking about the joys of being in recovery, I don't even know where to start. I mean, I've done a lot of growing and changing, like in the "relationships with men" area. I've done a lot of work connecting [my issues with men] with my childhood and my father and stuff around sex. I've seen a lot of behaviors around my wanting to "fix" men, and how it affects me today. When I'm acting out, wanting to be liked, and doing that people-pleasing routine, I'm looking at some major messed-up days. On days like that, serenity, man, is out the window. Suddenly, I'm bingeing on food, I'm "in my head," and feeling way uncomfortable again.

Now I'm dating a bunch of different people. I'm not sleeping with anyone. It's amazing. Everything I have today hinges on my being in recovery. Seriously, the job I have, the relationships I have at work, the friendships, the female friendships—I have *girl* friends, my sponsor… Everything rests on being clean! They want me to be in management training at work. They want *me* to be in *management!*

I've been working on my Fourth Step for months. I have notebooks and notebooks full. My sponsor's going to need a few days [to hear my story]. I'm pretty much doing Step work every day. Like right now, I'm doing a fear inventory—

where my fears come from, how they paralyze me, how they affect my life. After that, I'm doing assets; then I'm done. I can't believe it.

In my life, a lot of stuff will come up, and I tell myself, "I'm powerless over this, and what am I going to do? I'm going to believe in a higher power, and I'm going to turn it over. Okay? Cool..." A lot of it is becoming aware of how much I don't like myself, and working on liking myself, accepting myself, maintaining my self-esteem, and staying "out of my head," because that's a dangerous place, man. Also, realizing I have a choice today. I'm powerless over the first thought, but after that I have a choice, and I can turn it over. I tell you something, I like myself way better than when I first got into this program. There's still a lot of stuff there, but it's amazing, I was nowhere near as open, wise, or spiritual as I thought I was. I'm very slowly becoming the person I want to be. I'm very slowly coming to like the person I am, and that's cool.

None of that would be happening if I wasn't clean. I can't even imagine how fast the shit would hit the fan if I started using again. I can't imagine how much I'd stand to throw out if I used again. I hardly ever get drug hunger. The obsession has really been lifted. Geez, man, I have more money now than I think I've ever had. Regular income, and I'm saving for a car...

My relationship with God, my Higher Power, that has been phenomenal! When I'm not in a relationship with God, I'm "gone," I've "moved away." If I want to come back, I can. It's up to me. I've gotten so many gifts from God in this program so far—I'm so blessed, I really am. I'm so taken care of. I can ask for help and I get it, especially if I say I'm really dense and I need a big sign. Every time I'm in God's will, I get something out of it, I grow. There are so many miracles happening.

My mom has been an awesome support, awesome. In November she helped me learn I have a choice about how I was seeing myself. She said something like, "You're seeing [your problems] and you're going right over to pound on yourself instead of being nice to yourself for at least seeing reality." She's been incredible, just incredible!

With Jeanne, it's been up and down. But when we click, because we're both in recovery, it's like, "Wow, right on!" It couldn't get any better. We'll both be talking and saying how incredible this is.

Without the relationships I have in this program, I don't think I'd be able to do it. I don't even think God and I could do it alone.

CHAPTER THREE
Jeremy

Age 19
College Student
Ten Months of Sobriety

I had a pretty happy childhood, really. I got along with my folks pretty well—more so with my mother. I felt like I could talk to her about anything. My dad was real rough on me and my brother. We were kind of intimidated by him. He would yell a lot, but he never really hurt us much, except when we were real young. He hit us a few times then. My brother and I had our little fights and stuff, but I guess we were pretty close when we were young. He's eighteen months older than me. We shared a room and hung out together for awhile, but by sixth or seventh grade we were drifting apart.

We lived in this small town about an hour or so east of San Francisco until I was starting seventh grade. I liked it a lot. People were pretty much down to earth. It was like a little country town. You knew people and they knew you. The last two years we were trying to sell our house and commuting to school about 25 minutes away. My parents wanted to move to Pleasant Valley because the school system was better there. They didn't mean for us to commute that long, but it took two years to sell the house. That was a tough time, because I began to feel like I didn't fit anywhere.

I liked where we were living, and I didn't like the new place so much. Once I was going to school there for awhile, I lost some of my old friends because I was never around, and I had trouble making new friends because I couldn't stick around to play. My attitude was probably pretty lousy because I was upset about moving. Before that, I remember being real happy.

We finally moved when I was in seventh grade. Then I lost all my old friends. The first person I met out here was one of the people I started "using" with. I drank a few times. I had experimented a few times before, like half a beer in fifth grade, but I hadn't liked it. My brother did. In seventh grade, I started taking wine from our fridge every once in awhile. It was fun to be sneaky like that. Alcohol was, like, really macho, so it was a big thing. I don't think alcohol got me "high." It was more a fun thing to do.

Towards the middle of seventh grade, I switched friends again and hung out with the "using" crowd. I was curious. I knew they were doing it, and I wanted to be as cool as they were. I wanted to feel like I was a part of them. This one day I knew they were doing it, so I smoked pot with them. That was the first time I had gotten high. I liked it. I liked it a lot! Usually people don't get stoned their first time, but I think I did. After I smoked that once, I had it in my mind that I was a pot smoker. I thought I was cool and stuff, that I fit in. The whole idea of it got me to feel good.

In the spring of seventh grade I broke my leg, and that slowed me down for awhile. When it healed, for some reason I went back to my first friends in Pleasant Valley and started drinking more frequently—two to four times a week. Some of the alcohol was from parents' cabinets, but we discovered someone's wine cellar in an old bomb shelter. That kept us going for awhile. It was pretty old wine. Probably pretty good stuff. During that time I only smoked pot every once in a while.

I did that for awhile. Then I had a falling-out with one of my drinking buddies. By the beginning of eighth grade, I was hanging out with my "using" friends again. After I got really stoned one time, it was, like, set that I was going to be a stoner. I started using a lot—three to five times a week. Then every other week or so, I'd smoke every day. I stole some money, but mostly used my allowance for it. I was buying it from peers and older people. I really idolized people who sold pot. I was thinking I could be as cool as they were. Everyone looked up to them—the "old stoners."

It wasn't so much the feeling from smoking that was important; it was being cool, having that reputation. I always liked that it made me feel giggly and more at ease. I started smoking before school. One day the principal saw us and made us breathe into his face. I think he knew, but he couldn't prove it. He found the joint later, but he didn't do anything. That was the first time I thought I should stop. I think I even stopped for a month or so. But then one day, it was a spontaneous thing—I said, "Oh, well," and went back to smoking.

In ninth grade I started smoking at school, making it more a part of my life. I got into some trouble. Nothing really happened. Once we were suspended for five days, because we were caught drinking beer at a football game. It didn't change my thinking at all.

Probably midway through the year, I was getting bored with the same old thing. A new friend was really into acid, and he got me started on that. I liked that a lot! To me it was, like, more intensified than marijuana. I never really "tripped" that hard—just saw trails and patterns in the air. Sometimes we'd go into Berkeley and buy a sheet on the streets. I knew we were taking a gamble, that it could be bad stuff, but I did it anyway. After about four or five months of using LSD every weekend, I got bored with it, too. It had been totally fun, but when it made me start thinking about my feelings, I started using it way less.

Around that time, I met another new friend who got me started on crank [speed]. I didn't like it the first couple of times, but I kept trying. After the third time, I liked it a lot! I could talk to anyone. I could think about anything. I could do anything. I think I did it once every week or two, except during finals week in ninth grade when I did it every day. That summer I tried cocaine and nitrous, but didn't like them very much.

By tenth grade I was back to smoking pot regularly. It was the drug that made me feel better. Everything else was too intense. Pot was always the "kick back and feel euphoric" thing. I'd wake up, take a hit, smoke some at lunch, smoke some when I got home; cheap stuff. I kept on doing that basically most of the year.

I guess looking back on it, while I was using I thought drug education didn't really apply to me. It certainly didn't apply to pot. Maybe harder stuff, but, since I wasn't doing anything harder any more, I kind of blew off anything we were told. Besides, I thought I knew a lot about drugs from my experiences, but I didn't know anything, really. It certainly never entered my head when we were getting high.

I didn't think marijuana was harming me in any way. I always thought, as long as I could be nice and not create too much of a disturbance, everything was fine. In my mind my brother was being an asshole. I knew he was far worse than me. He was always fighting with my parents. I never really thought pot was affecting my relationship with my parents. I guess it did, though, because I was keeping secrets and lying to them. I always made it a point to be nice to them, no matter what was happening to me. I was always the quieter one, so it was easier for me to cover things up with my parents and make things seem all right. I probably got away with a lot more, because I appeared okay. In my mind I was smoking marijuana because it was more fun than not using. I sure didn't see any problems with it until one day...

My brother went into a rehab program in late winter of my sophomore year. It was pretty intense. He was an inpatient, and we had to go all day on Saturday and on Thursday night to this family program. I was still smoking—no problem here. My parents didn't know. I said I had used a few times, but didn't presently use. At the last family session, the day before my brother was getting out, he confronted me and said, "You're using, and I think you need some help, too." I guess all the while he was in treatment, he had been telling my parents I was using regularly, but it took them till that last night to confront me. Maybe they could only handle so much at once.

I tried to deny what he said by saying I wasn't using regularly. I rationalized my lying by saying to myself, "I'll stop now if I just don't have to go to rehab." I meant I'd quit. I didn't feel bad or guilty for lying right to their faces, even after weeks of hearing lectures about the disease and how it distorts your thinking. I was still into that marijuana justifying and rationalizing crap. I really thought I could stop right away if I could just get out of there.

But they made me stay. I was in the inpatient program for a twelve-day assessment. At first I didn't buy the fact that I had a problem. I started buying into it a little bit after about a week. By then my brain was getting a little clear. I learned a lot in those twelve days. At the end, the staff thought I'd do okay in the outpatient program, so I went to that every day for about a year and a half. In addition to my program, I still went to the weekly multifamily group for my brother's aftercare.

I started getting into it. I'd go to meetings with my brother. We were both clean. We'd hang out together. He'd drive me around. Neither one of us had friends at first. I started making new friends when I was in the outpatient program. I liked my new friends. I guess I liked being honest with myself and with other people. Instead of seeing myself like an ordinary stoner, I started seeing myself above them, because I didn't need to use to have fun. I liked being clean and sober. Like, I started hiking and mountain biking, stuff I never thought of doing when I was getting high. All I ever thought of doing when I was getting high was something like looking at stars, but I really started doing things when I was sober.

As treatment dropped off for me, I started going to more meetings. Then my brother graduated and left for school about a year after I went through the program. I was still going to that multifamily group once a week, but we finally agreed I didn't need to go any more. I'd been going to two or three A.A. or N.A. meetings a week, and I'd worked up to the Sixth Step with a sponsor. But then I stopped doing them. I don't know why.

I think it was right around that same time, about two years after I was out of rehab, I was going to community college and had run into one of my old "using" friends. He had asked me several times, and finally I was thinking, "Yeah, I could just go back to my regular life," so I smoked with him. But all the while I was supposedly getting high, this stuff was going through my head, "Should I tell? Should I tell? I don't need this, I've been working too hard for this.

I don't need this." It wasn't like it used to be. It wasn't about me needing to fit in that time. I only used that one time. It was real scary, and I felt very guilty. In those few minutes, I blew two years and almost three months of sobriety. Right after that, I went to a meeting and told.

After that, I hit a lot more meetings. I started talking to a lot of people. I got into it a little more for a while, then gradually slowed down to maybe one a week, then one every other week. That's basically how it's been since then.

I'm still at that same community college. It's basically like finishing high school. I haven't seen much of that old friend. We haven't been in classes together. I'm only taking two courses, and working. Most people here go to school, learn, and leave. I don't see a lot of partying. It was a lot harder not to use in high school, a lot harder! It's always tough, but at least it's a little easier than it was.

It scares me sometimes that I've only gone through six of the Twelve Steps. I always go to the same meetings, mostly young people's meetings. I'd like to finish the Steps, but...
I have a Higher Power, but I choose not to see God as my Higher Power. It's just somebody up there. Spirituality isn't a tremendously big part of my recovery. I never got into it that much. I use it, but only when I think I need to use it. But when I need to use a higher power, it's there. I definitely have a Higher Power in a sense, because I know I could never do this all by myself. But I'm just not sure about it.

In the beginning, it was difficult for me to come to grips with my being an addict. I was so much into being a "user" that I wasn't seeing myself as an addict. That was really hard for me. I thought I was just an abuser, but then I found out I was a big-time addict. I don't have that out-of-control feeling that I need to use anymore. If something feels out of control, I talk about it at a meeting, or I use my Higher

Power and pray. Talking it out helps the most. It's been almost a year since I relapsed. I'm more sure than ever before that I don't want to use. I guess I needed that relapse to find out what it was really like and to find out what I really wanted. I guess it's a matter of finding out what's right for you and staying with the program, whether or not you go to meetings or read A.A. books. You've just got to keep it as an important part of your life.

Mostly, I hang out with people who hardly use. A few acquaintances are in the program. Unfortunately, I've seen a lot of my old treatment buddies go back out and stay out there. Most of my friends aren't in the program, but they're familiar with it. They've gone to meetings with me.

I definitely feel like I have a better relationship with my parents, now. I get along a lot better with my dad. They both learned a lot in the family program in rehab. They've changed. I'm more honest with them both. I feel more casual about talking to them, although I never told them about my relapse. I guess I keep my program to myself. It would be nice if they were more involved in the program, but it's up to them.

What do I like about being clean and sober? Basically not needing to use. Before it was a regular thing. I feel a lot "higher" not using than I felt from using. I just feel like I don't need it. I like doing natural things, like hiking and mountain biking. I never would have done those things if I were still using. I like doing things a lot better than when I was just sitting around and getting high. In sobriety I've learned to do things and not just look at things.

My only goal right now is to stay sober as long as I can. I can't really picture myself that far down the road. I just know sobriety is really important to me. I feel more whole as a person now that I'm sober, more confident about myself and what I can do. I'm happy sober. That's basically what it boils down to. I'm happy. What else could you ask for?

CHAPTER FOUR
Howard

Age 47
Lawyer
One Year of Sobriety

M y mother was an alcoholic; my father was a "dry" drunk. I guess he did his share of drinking, and then quit. He did the classic white-knuckling for the rest of his life. He never had the benefits of the A.A. program. I didn't know that until I began my recovery program about four years ago. Before that I thought we just had a miserable family life.

My father was twenty-one, my mother eighteen, when I was born. My sister came along four years later. When I was growing up, my father was a jock and a good businessman. His reaction whenever he was mad was to beat me up. He did that regularly. My mother was this beautiful model. We were Jewish, but it wasn't a Jewish home in the classic sense at all. My father was an atheist. My mother liked to party. When they were married, she'd sleep with anyone. My father had one girlfriend all the way through, and then eventually married her. It was a terrible marriage. I was left alone a lot! They divorced soon after my bar mitzvah.

A typical situation that sums up my childhood occurred when I was nine. It was the moment that I lost whatever was left of my innocence. I went to a bowling party and never got picked up. My mother was supposed to have picked me up. Finally, I called my father at work. It was a Saturday. Was he ever mad! He came for me, and we went looking for my mother. We finally found her drinking in a bar with her friends. By the time we found her and my father yelled at her, I was in tears, but for some reason he didn't beat me that day. You know, she never apologized. She said she was entitled to be there with her friends.

In summary, my mother wasn't there for me before the divorce, and she wasn't there for me after the divorce. I wasn't "man enough" for my father. If there was a whole line-up of boys, I wouldn't have been the one he picked. As a kid, I felt the pain from never being the focus of either parent and never being "good enough."

At the Jewish holidays, Manischewitz kosher wines were served. That was the beginning of my drinking career. I was probably four, five, or six at the time. I liked the wine. I would always drink all that I could. I liked the buzz. I had a craving for it and looked forward to the holidays for the wine. My other early addiction was television. I watched tons of television, tons. I only had one close friend. I never did schoolwork. I was one of those kids the teachers would say things like, "He could be achieving so much more."

We lived in a fairly large city on the East Coast in the Jewish neighborhood, pretty affluent. I only knew one kid who had more money than we did. Part of our "affluence" was we had a summer home, only our summer home was in an area where everyone else lived year 'round. So I didn't have any friends there, because they had year 'round shared experiences, and I was always an outsider. When we'd come home, I was an outsider again, because I hadn't shared summer experiences with those kids. I was always the odd one out.

I was aware at the time of being different from everyone else. During all the time I was left alone, I developed these grandiose dreams and fantasies. I saw myself as being next-to-God, almost God-like, and that's why I didn't fit in with the kids around me. I wanted to be special to someone. God was my buddy, he was the only other one special enough to appreciate me. It wasn't connected to religion; I couldn't stand going to synagogue. One of the "leading" men of the synagogue was having an affair with my mother. (He was married at the time and so was she.) I couldn't stand the hypocrisy. The feeling of not fitting in anywhere continued through most of my life.

I began drinking regularly in high school. When I was 19 and a freshman in college, my roommates and I decided we were going to experiment with marijuana. Back in 1966, making a buy was a big deal, kind of like buying heroin. It was hard to get ahold of. My first time, my roommates and I were sitting in this bar. We knew this guy sitting at the bar sold it. I sneaked up to him, sure the entire FBI or police force was watching. I asked him if he was selling, and he said, "Yes." I told him I'd like to buy some marijuana, and he said, "Sure!" and he reached into his pocket to whip some out, and I said, "Oh no, not in here!" so we snuck into an alley. I had told my roommates, "If I don't come back in and he does, I'm going straight back to the apartment." They were supposed to meet me there.

Well, as soon as he gave it to me, I was ready to run back to the apartment, but he insisted I smell it for the quality. I didn't know anything; it could have been grass from someone's front yard. All I wanted was to get it in my pocket and race home.

When I got there, I was dying, my heart was pounding. I thought it was a major crime. I didn't dare get into any kind of trouble—my father would have killed me. I locked all the doors and made sure it was my roommates when I heard people coming. We closed all the blinds, went into a bedroom, shut the windows, put a lamp on the floor—the paranoia was incredible! We wanted to make sure nobody saw us.

I liked the high; no I *loved* the high, but I didn't like what it took to get there. I wasn't a cigarette smoker, so it took me a few times to learn how to get high without killing myself.

Within two weeks, we were out on our balcony smoking the stuff in broad daylight. We smoked as much as we could get until I transferred schools in 1967. We also did LSD when we could.

We'd go high to these drug meetings sponsored by the police department—this was really in the "reefer madness" days. They'd say once you smoke a couple of joints, then the next step is heroin. We knew that wasn't true. We had been smoking for months, we had no desire to use anything stronger, and LSD didn't count... I kept wondering, "Why are they making such a big deal of this stuff when it makes me feel so great?"

I had a 1.7 grade point average my first semester of college. The second year when I was smoking a lot of marijuana, I got a 3.0. It was proof that you could function on marijuana. I was in great shape! I was a good athlete. I wasn't getting drunk. (I had replaced drinking with marijuana.) I thought, "Everyone should be doing this stuff; it's great!" It was a whole culture, the *us* and the *them*. For once I fit in. I belonged. I was funny. It was neat.

I transferred schools to marry my high school sweetheart, probably the single biggest mistake of my life. We were married in 1969. Within six months, we were sitting in a counselor's office. I wanted out so badly; but she cried, and I said I'd stay.

After years of introspection, I've realized my first wife was a trophy; she was beautiful. Everyone had wanted her, and I got her, but she was a very cold, miserable person. I was stoned all the time and she was anorexic. Maybe she approved of my smoking because it kept us apart, and that was fine with her. It was awful—just like my parents' marriage.

Once, in about 1977, I remember sitting on the couch downstairs listening to music through headphones and smoking grass when I suddenly realized, "I'm doing the same thing tonight that I do every night. I get home from work, I eat an awful dinner that she reluctantly prepared, I come down here and get high and 'meditate.' " (That's what I called it.) Friday nights, friends got together and got high all night. (Some wives joined us; mine didn't.) Saturdays, my wife joined us, and we'd smoke. (It got to be Saturdays during the days, also.) I thought I was "more loose" when I was high, so Sundays before tennis, I'd get high. I thought I could experience *it* (whatever it was) more deeply if I was high. That sense still haunts me.

That was the only time until A.A. I thought there was a problem It was the only time I realized my whole life was about getting high. I decided to quit. I announced it to my friends. They didn't really want to hear it. I didn't belong again. My sobriety lasted about two weeks. I went back to smoking again and thinking people who didn't smoke were total assholes. How could you possibly enjoy life if you didn't get high?

For twenty-five years, before I did anything, I'd get high. When I smoked grass, I was *there* with Einstein and all the great artists of our time, and I truly *could* get into life. In contrast, when I'd get drunk, I'd get sloppy, my thoughts weren't clear, I was out of control, and there was no telling what I'd do.

I'd get high in my car, because it was easier to deal with traffic. I sometimes swapped services for grass or bought from my clients, but I never got high during the day if I had to go to court or file papers, but there were times... I just lived with knowing it was okay to smoke pot.

Up until four years ago, when I went to my first Codependents Anonymous (CODA) meeting and began my recovery program, I blamed myself for how my parents treated me. I believed I wasn't good enough; I had it coming to me. I was always the last kid picked for team sports; I was nothing. I always felt my father was justified in beating me. Even after law school when I was a star, nationally known, handling some sensational cases, very well respected in my field, it was never enough. My parents never acknowledged it. If you were to ask my parents, they'd know I was a lawyer, but if you were to ask them "What type of law does he practice?" they would have no idea.

Over the years, the pot got stronger, but it didn't do as much for me as it used to. I'd still smoke and take a walk, because I couldn't enjoy trees and birds without being high. But at times I'd be driving along, getting high, and wondering, "What's wrong? I'm not getting as high as I used to; I need to be higher than this."

I never felt like I belonged on the East Coast. The only two years in my life I had been really happy were my first two years in college. I struggled through nine years in my first marriage. In the end we were in counseling. After four sessions the therapist said she could not see how we stayed together, since we had absolutely nothing in common. We split shortly thereafter. I then got involved with Linda. We married a year later. I had a lot of pleasure in the early years of our marriage, but I was never happy where we were living, which is where I had grown up. I dealt with my discomfort by smoking dope and using LSD when I could get it. One morning at the height of my midlife crisis, I asked Linda if we could sell everything and move. She agreed.

After we moved, I lost all our money in a bad business venture with a friend who was like a brother. In retrospect, I think I was screwed up from drugs, codependence, and incest issues. I don't know what the pot and my desire to belong, to be part of a family contributed; and how did all that put me in a partnership with someone whom I should have just stayed friends with? Was it the pot affecting my judgment, or was it me wanting a brother and carrying him financially for eighteen months? My codependence? My drugs? I can't separate out all the factors.

When we moved here, we met a professional crowd that smoked. My life was not pleasant by any stretch of the imagination. The people I was involved with at work were driving me crazy. All I thought about during the day was getting high. On the weekends, I connected with my pot-smoking buddies, and we floated the time away. I smoked when I could around the house. As my son got older, I went from smoking in my basement office to the bathroom, garage, car—I did not want him to smell the odor.

After Linda was disabled in a car accident and I almost lost a second business, I started going to CODA meetings. From there I literally stumbled onto ACA (Adult Children of Alcoholics) meetings. I was a member of a health club, and they had ACA meetings. I thought, "How nice! I can work out and go to a meeting at the same place." The stories I heard sounded familiar and hit home. From there I went to Incest Survivors meetings, Al-Anon, and finally, in 1992, to an open A.A. meeting. I didn't think I needed A.A., but I wanted a Step Study meeting, and it was at a convenient place and time, so I went.

I didn't think I had an addiction problem with either drugs or alcohol. It was suggested that I clear all the pot and alcohol out of the house. I did not think it was a problem, so I agreed. I was out of grass at the time, so I assembled the booze into a box and was going to throw it away. I then thought, "It's a shame to just give away all this stuff." So I started to drink it. I finished off about a pint and picked up another bottle. I got very frightened.

Fortunately, I had some A.A. friends, and I called one, and I kept talking about how I was drinking. People in A.A. won't tell you if you have a problem or not. I didn't really believe I was an alcoholic and addict, but I guess I was wondering about it. I knew a therapist, and she said, "The fact that you've been smoking pot every day for twenty-five years might tell you a little something about whether you have a problem or not." She advised, "What you ought to do is go to a closed A.A. meeting and see what it feels like." I went to a meeting, and I introduced myself as an alcoholic and addict, even though I did not believe it. It took me a few more weeks of listening to people's stories to convince myself. Then I started looking at my own drug addiction.

Because of "the marijuana maintenance program," I learned, I hadn't needed to drink all those years. In other words, if it hadn't been for pot, I probably would have been a gutter alcoholic. I just liked marijuana more and had switched my addiction at nineteen. It was a cleaner drug; you didn't wake up hung over; you didn't have to smoke all night, just a joint every few hours. There was no evidence pot was addictive, therefore [I believed] it wasn't. I believed if you stuck to pot, you weren't an addict. And I could go a long time without drinking, so I wasn't an alcoholic. That was my denial at work in me during all those years. After all, I had always been more philosophical, capable of deeper insights, and I could really get into talking about life when I was stoned.

After being in A.A. for six or seven weeks, I went away on business. My client had a bottle of wine put in my room. I had such cravings! Of course I didn't have my substitute [marijuana] for the first time, and I absolutely went crazy that whole night. By the end of that night I knew that when I had substituted "the marijuana maintenance program" for alcohol, I hadn't avoided a problem; I had created a double addiction. I got very serious about my A.A. program and recovering from my own addictions after that.

What have I gotten in recovery? My life, my marriage. I don't hit my son any more or blow up the way I used to all the time with him. I'm able to turn a lot of the stuff over to God and try to make the little decisions myself, leaving the big ones to God.

Right now I'm caught in this bureaucracy, and have been for months. It may cost me my biggest contract. My cash flow is horrendous! If this client disappears, the cornerstone of my financial success is in jeopardy, but I'm not panicked today. Sometimes I get panicked and then I meditate or go to meetings, and I'm okay. It's totally out of my control. I pray, asking God to give me the strength to accept whatever decision is made. I wouldn't have done that before. I'd try to take control and figure out what kind of influence I could exert, what I should do. I'd be all involved, but now I know I have other people fighting for me, so there's nothing I can do except sit back and wait. That's all I can do. I couldn't have done that a year ago. Now I'm doing what's in front of me and letting them and God do the rest.

What happened to God for all those years after he had been my buddy when I was little? First of all, it was alcohol, pot, or God, and I had the first two. But there's something else very important: When I was nineteen, I was swimming one day. I was really a good swimmer, but I came so close to death that day. I was really drowning, and what I did was, I prayed to God and said, "If you save my life, I will never ask for anything else again." I came to the surface, and I was right off the beach. I had no strength left. Had I not been so close, I wouldn't have made it. I kept that promise until I was 43 or 44 years old and in recovery.

Since being in the program, I feel differently. I don't feel like I'm the center of the universe anymore. It's so much more free. I don't feel like I have all the responsibility. I'm learning this sense of humility. I can't fix you, but maybe I can share my experience, strength, and hope, and that can help you, but I can't do much.

That experience of almost drowning—I've come to realize my bargain didn't save my life; God saved my life. He didn't need my promise. If it was his will that I drown, do you think I could have convinced him otherwise? And that experience is helping me today. It's going to be God's will one way or the other.

Now, when I have reservations about something, I meditate, and a message from God comes, like, "Go to a meeting and just listen." The last time that happened, I went to a meeting and heard a man share, "I do what's in front of me and do the best thing I can. Everything else is the will of God." I needed to hear that that night. It helped me a lot. Those are gifts of the program.

I have a curiosity about what [sexual abuse] happened between my mother and me. I know more will be revealed. And I know God doesn't give us more than we can take; I'll have the tools when the going gets tough.

When I used to get high, I'd get these profound thoughts, but the next morning I couldn't remember the details. Now I can remember details. Yet every once in awhile, I think, maybe if I got high this would be better. Like, on a bad skiing day, I've thought, "If only I had some pot, I could get into the rhythm; it's all timing." If I'm not going to relapse, I have to see that as drug hunger. It comes with the disease, but I don't have to act on it.

I'm lucky or something, because I have support around me. People know I'm in recovery. They don't offer me pot. People respect my recovery. They're glad I have my sobriety. It's all about selection; I've selected people who are supportive of me, now. I don't speak to my parents; it's been four years since I talked to my mother and two years since I talked to my father. I've needed that distance. I don't want to be self-destructive anymore. Oh, two weeks ago I had the best party—no drugs—to celebrate my one-year birthday of being clean and sober. I feel great! And it's only just beginning.

CHAPTER FIVE
Josh

Age 19
College Student
Four Years of Sobriety

I grew up in Southern California near the beach. I had my first drink of alcohol when I was four years old. It was vodka punch, and I liked it a lot. When I was five years old, I was molested by a female baby-sitter, and I knew then I was different from other kids. I think I had always felt different, but that really added to my feelings of being different from other kids. I'm an Asian American, and I think that also fed into my feelings of being different. Other Asian kids got teased and ridiculed. I didn't want any part of being Asian for as long as I can remember. I don't think I got teased as much as other Asian kids, maybe because I tried so hard not be Asian. I didn't want to be unusual. I'm just now getting used to the fact I'm Asian; it's still pretty hard.

I don't know how it started, but from an early age I looked up to the party crowd. I saw movies as a kid, like *Fast Times at Ridgemont High*, and I looked up to the in-crowd, the party crowd—all that action. I looked up to kids old enough to smoke pot and I couldn't wait. I wanted that fast-action lifestyle. It looked particularly fun. I had always been involved in a lot of action.

55

I had a lot of energy as a kid. I couldn't sit still. I had a short attention span. I was always getting into trouble for that. I was raised getting hit a lot for things that I had no control over, like not sitting still, not paying attention, things like that.

As a kid, I was always trying to make a buck. We lived in an area where all the other kids had really good quality things. I was quite materialistic. My parents would buy me a bike from K-Mart. It wasn't that they didn't have the money for a brand name. My father just didn't get that it was important; he was Asian. I wanted a name-brand bike like the other kids. I wanted the kinds of things I saw all the other kids have. So I was always selling things. I bought a BB gun, used it for a while; another kid wanted it, so I sold it to him and made a little profit. Then I went out and bought a better BB gun. I was always doing things like that. I wanted to be as good as the other kids. I wanted to be number one.

By the fourth grade, I was listening to heavy metal rock-and-roll like Quiet Riot, Ozzy Osborne, Def Leppard; I looked up to that rocker lifestyle. I had a hard time with attention deficit disorder when I was a kid; I even had to go to resource classes for a short while. But I could listen to rock-and-roll for a long time.

I never could talk to my mom and dad. They were Asian, very Asian, and I didn't want anything to do with them, because I didn't want anything to do with being Asian. So I never did things with them. Somehow I was ashamed of being Asian. I never wanted to be seen with them. I never could talk to them.

I never wanted to be weak, and somehow I never wanted to have emotions. I could never get angry, because being angry meant I'd be weak; I never wanted to let my defenses down.

By the end of sixth grade, I was experimenting with alcohol occasionally, drinking from my parents' liquor cabinet, dipping into my father's gallon bottles. He never noticed it. I'd never tell, and pretended I didn't like liquor, so they wouldn't take it away or notice I was drinking. My father drank every night; I never noticed that until right before I went into rehab.

In seventh grade, I'd have shots of Jack Daniels in the morning every once in awhile. On the outside, I was a happy-go-lucky kid. I had three goals that year: (1) I wanted to get good grades so my parents would get off my back; (2) I wanted to be with the party crowd; and (3) I wanted to body board. I didn't really start drinking heavily until ninth grade.

I started smoking pot the summer between seventh and eighth grades. It was 1985. I got the pot from an older guy across the street. He said, "Want to get high?" "Yes!" I said. In public school, I had tried rolling joints of chives and parsley—I couldn't wait—so when he asked me, I was ready!

Before Christmas of my freshman year, I was smoking pot on a daily basis by myself. Sometime between eighth grade and ninth grade, I started body boarding, and I was getting good. My grades even improved. Pot seemed to help me study, and I had started getting into the fast lifestyle I had wanted. I think I thought if I was a go-getter and moved fast enough, people wouldn't notice I was Asian, because I still didn't want to be Asian. Right around that time, just as I was getting all my dreams, I was told we'd be moving at the end of the school year up to Northern California, to San Francisco. I was really excited. San Francisco—I had heard there was a lot of action up there.

When my parents told me we'd be moving, I made my first pledge to myself about pot. I told myself I'd party really hard the rest of the year and then leave it all behind me in Southern California when we moved. I was buying my pot with the $20 allowance I got each week, whatever other money I was making, and sharing with friends. We could get a fat joint for $2 in those days, and it didn't take a lot to get me stoned because I was still starting out. I hadn't built up any kind of tolerance. After making the pledge, I did party hard.

Pot was my main drug, but I tried everything that came my way. My goal was to try every drug there was. I never had any reservations about doing drugs. "Yes, let's do it all" was my philosophy. I even tried PCP and, although it was a scary experience, if I could have gotten more, I would have used it again.

At the end of the school year, we moved up to a *suburb* of San Francisco, and I was bummed. I thought we were moving to San Francisco. This suburb was about an hour's drive away from the city. I had cows in my backyard. There was no beach for body boarding. I had no friends. I wasn't talking with my family. I was miserable! My first memory of living up here was going to a restaurant with my parents and getting teased. I absolutely hated this place. I felt so humiliated outside that restaurant. I felt like it was the end of the world. I kept that inside a long time! I had brought an ounce of pot with me, and there I was, 14 years old, smoking that ounce of pot and needing more.

I got a job making $5 an hour that summer. At work I met a guy who was in his second year of college, and he connected me with drugs. I tried cocaine. On my fifteenth birthday, I went to this all-day rock concert, with bands like Van Halen, Metallica, and Kingdom Come. It was a drug supermarket. I bought some LSD there and brought it home. I didn't know what to expect, except what I had seen in the movies—different colors and guys going "Wow!" I took my first acid at 9 A.M. one day, and I was tripping until 3 A.M. I wanted to die. I almost committed suicide; I had the razor to my wrist. I didn't have anybody to talk to, and I didn't know how to calm myself down, but I tried it again a while later.

That summer I started really fighting with my parents. I thought it was all their fault that I had to move, and that I was Asian. I didn't want anything to do with them. I'd fight with my younger brother a lot, too. He was eight years younger than me, and my parents would often fight with me because I was fighting with him. They seemed to assume that because I was older I should have known better. They'd always stick up for him, no matter what. He never got into trouble. He didn't have any of the same kind of energy or attention problems I had. He never got hit, and I had always gotten hit when I was in trouble. I'd get hit because I couldn't sit down, or I couldn't sit still. He never had those problems. There was a lot of jealousy involved in my fighting with him.

By the time I was fifteen, all my dreams were going downhill. I'd work, come home, get high, and go to sleep and dream. I was king of my dream world. Ever since I was a kid, I used to work really hard at controlling my dreams, thinking before I fell asleep of what I wanted to dream about, these elaborate fantasies. I got pretty good at that. I had a pretty good imagination. My dream world was my escape. And that's what I did that summer—worked, got high, slept, and dreamed.

Oh, yeah, I also thought I had to have a woman, which I didn't have. I placed a lot of *me* on what other people thought, and I didn't have *her*, so I felt like I was no good.

That next year in school, my sophomore year, I didn't have any energy; the zest for life I had was gone. I couldn't participate in life anymore; I wasn't going anywhere. I was so depressed, I wanted to die. I was just afraid to do it. I was smoking pot all the time. I was so depressed, I'd sleep a lot. For about two years I tried to moderate my pot usage, and I couldn't do it. My whole life was a pile of shame, and I couldn't talk to anyone. My only escape was getting high and sleeping.

During that school year, I tried hooking up with the clean-cut kids. But at home, I had tons of paraphernalia, and I started smoking pot in the mornings. Everything started going downhill. I'd fall asleep in class. My grade point went down to 2.5, and then, the last semester, 1.6. I was fighting with my parents all the time. I couldn't remember what day of the week it was. I was getting loaded from morning until night when I finally fell asleep.

I joined a ski club that winter; then I couldn't smoke from Saturday until Sunday night. That worked for ski season, but then it was back to partying. I'd read *High Times* like a bible. I started obsessing on drugs. I didn't have a girlfriend that whole year.

Right around April, I wanted to die. I was miserable. I didn't care about anything. I fantasized how I was going to die. I couldn't reach out. I couldn't connect with anybody. I was real lonely, and I tried to numb it out with pot. I'd sit in my room with the door shut and smoke pot, listen to heavy metal rock-and-roll, and sleep. That was my life. The last three months, I started doing LSD, too. The fights with my parents started getting violent. I'd have nail marks from my mother. They'd throw things at me, or throw me around. I was doing so much drugs; it was a cry for help. They were oblivious until those last three months; then they drug-tested me. It was such a miserable time. I even did a lot of cocaine during that time. They'd deliver it to my doorstep. I had dreams about smoking crack. I tried to make it twice, but I messed it up. I'd stare at a friend's needles who had diabetes, and dream about stealing them and shooting cocaine. My sole mission in life was to follow the Grateful Dead around and do as many drugs as I could.

I lost all hope, all drive, all my old dreams. I had been paranoid, had anxiety attacks from the drugs, but that didn't slow me down. I had to have things a certain way or my heart would race, and I knew it was the end of the world. I had to have music and food, and I thought I'd go crazy if I didn't have it exactly when I wanted it. I thought I was going crazy—like a drug-induced schizophrenia.

On July 17, 1989, two days before my sixteenth birthday, my parents told me they wanted me to go to a counseling session. The counseling session was at a rehab unit for teenagers but I didn't know that when I agreed to go. The counselor asked me what my definition of a drug addict was, and I said, "Someone who does drugs every day." There was no question in my mind that I was a drug addict; it was the only thing I could do right. I agreed to enter the program right from the interview. I didn't even go back home to pack up my things; my parents brought them later. I knew immediately I'd be there the whole 45 days.

I had never been able to bond with other males as a kid in sports. I didn't have good eye-hand coordination, so any sport involving a ball, I was no good at. The only thing I had been good at was body boarding and later, skiing. I had lost the body boarding when we moved to Northern California.

When I lost that, the only thing I could take pride in was getting the best and cheapest drugs.

When I entered rehab, I knew from that first day I didn't like how I was living. I knew this might be the only chance I'd get. I saw rehab as my chance—my only chance. I didn't know if it would work, but I made a decision to try not to fight it. I was the only weird one in treatment, not fighting it.

Rehab also provided a buffer between me and my parents. I was happy to be there, away from my parents. I thought at first they were the problem. So I was happy. I didn't think my family was right. We didn't talk. We weren't close. I felt a connection in rehab with other people. I didn't feel so lonely anymore. I liked rehab.

I started going to meetings. The first person I saw speak at a meeting was a woman who talked about partying hard. She had *had* what I [thought I] had wanted. She talked about feeling miserable and wanting to die. I said, "Yeah!" I connected with her. It clicked.

I didn't know exactly what it felt like to be sober, but I was going to give it a try. I hadn't known what it was like to be high at first, and I had gotten used to that. I was hoping I could get used to being sober. When I got home after the 45-day program, I gave all my stash to my parents. It had been hidden in quite a few places, so I knew that if they had searched my room while I was gone, they couldn't have found it all. I rounded it all up and gave it to them.

I did what I was supposed to do. Whatever they (my counselors or people in A.A.) told me to do, I did. I was feeling much better than I had in so long. I went to a lot of meetings. I got a sponsor. I was working the Steps. I did service a lot. Meetings got me out of the house. But at first, I was doing the A.A. program and taking the expression "take what you like and leave the rest" very seriously.

Oh, yeah, I remember going to a wedding with my parents when I was newly sober. It was the first thing I had done with them in so long. My dad was drinking a lot! Right after the wedding, he handed me a drink to give to the groom. I couldn't believe that; it was such a slippery place for me to be in the first place. We talked about that in family aftercare, and the rehab staff contracted with my father that he had to go to A.A. and take the liquor out of the house. I guess my parents had been able to ignore my drug problem for a long time partly because of his problem. And I never really noticed how much he drank until right before I went into rehab. I had just appreciated the big bottles being around for years and the fact that they never noticed anything missing.

When I was in the program about a year, I met a girl in Alateen. I had never felt particularly close to anyone in my life, and she became everything to me. I even quit going to meetings as much. She and I were together all the time! After about eight months, I drove her out of my life by putting too much on her. Then I was really miserable, angry, and hurt. I'd wake up angry and stay angry all day, going to bed still angry. It was a real hard time, but it got me back to what I needed to do to stay sober, and I didn't use because of it.

I got a new sponsor, went to meetings every day; I was desperate again. I worked the Steps, but I didn't "take what I like and leave the rest" this time. I really worked the Steps and did things on a regular basis. After that my life got better.

Before the end of my senior year, life seemed to click. I graduated from high school. I hadn't done very well; I guess

I got bored with it. And then I started college at the local junior college.

My life has improved! My dreams, my hopes are coming true. Now I can talk with my mom about my day, about meetings. School is going really well. I show up and participate in life, and I couldn't do that when I was loaded. The amazing thing is, there's no way I could have done what I'm doing today back when I was using. I started college slowly last year, just a few credits, and working. This year I've taken full loads and worked both semesters. Everything seems to have worked out. I'm even about to move out of my parents' house and into a house with two other guys in the program. I've never had to go back out there and try [drugs] again. I have almost five years of sobriety.

Every once in awhile, I think, "What if it was only a phase?" I've seen other young people party hard [with drugs] for a while, and then seem okay. But then I say, "No, I'm an alcoholic and an addict. I can't drink normally. I can't smoke pot normally, and if I start again, I can't participate in life."

It's strange, too—I'm young… I only drank and used hard for two years, but I have to remember I'm still an addict—it just went quickly for me. I'm glad I was at such a desperate point when I got to rehab, because I wanted something to be different!

It's amazing, because I meet really nice people now. I thought being sober would limit my life, but it hasn't. I have a lot of fun. still go to concerts, but I bring a lot of sober people with me. Life is good! I go to a lot of A.A. dances. I rarely go to "big parties" like I used to dream about. And if I go at all, I bring sober friends with me. When I was newly sober, I had to take a break and get a spiritual base before I could go to concerts or an occasional party. In my fourth year, I really started getting into spirituality more—meditating on a regular basis.

My life isn't perfect. I've made mistakes, and that's what the Tenth Step is about—learning from your mistakes.

I'm still that striver, that go-getter, but I'm learning I don't have to be the best. I try to be the best I can be, not the best-of-the-best. I really love deep conversations with friends where we analyze life, and my friends and I get together and have "bonding" experiences. I couldn't ever do that before.

A lot of the last year has been learning how to do school better and trying to get out of community college with good enough grades to transfer to a good state school. I've been working on getting balance in my life. I've been getting more confidence, feeling better about myself. If I can take care of my emotional stuff, I can concentrate and focus more on school. It all kind of relates.

I guess I work a lot on how to manage my stress. I read through the *Big Book* a couple of pages at a time, and then I read it again. I go to meetings. I drink herbal tea. I sit, meditate, and pray. I make an effort to calm myself down when I need to. Life is good!

CHAPTER SIX

Dan

Age 54
Physician
Six Years of Sobriety

My grandparents lost their farm in the Midwest during the Dust Bowl era, moved West, and became farm workers. They settled in a small farming community in California. During the Depression, they were very poor, but maintained their pride. I begin my story back then, because I think some of the messages I heard from my mother, who was very bright and really wanted to improve herself, were a direct result of her background. She described certain embarrassments, like, when she and her family would go into the fields and try to work overtime, so they could buy a house. The boss would say, "What can you do?" My grandmother would say, "We'll do anything." When I was growing up, my mother would say, "Never say you'll do anything; say you're somebody—like a doctor."

So I got the message that I came from a poor background, but had to be somebody. My grandmother and aunts worked overtime to send my mother to nursing school. After nursing school, my mother settled in a larger town in the valley. My dad worked for the railroad.

My mother got cancer when I was four. This had a very devastating effect, because we were a very close-knit family, and they had planned on having more children. She received life-saving nitrogen mustard chemotherapy that had just become available. It prolonged her life, but we went into a pattern of, every time she would get treatments, there was always the possibility that she would die. The only treatment available was in Los Angeles. She would get sick, my parents would leave, and I would stay with my aunt. Her debilitation from the chemotherapy would last two, three, four weeks. When I was with my aunt, I had to go to a different school, so my life was one of isolation, loneliness. I never questioned what was happening; I knew to just go along with their comings and goings. There was an aura of death in our house, but it was at the time when you didn't talk about death. I remember talking to my uncle years later and asking why I wasn't told that she could die, and he said, "Well, we didn't talk about death back then."

I felt lonely, alienated, and different. But what I found out was that I could prove myself and have some sense of self through accomplishments. So I worked very hard through sports. I had success in sports, but I wasn't a natural athlete. For example, I would practice hour after hour on my basketball shots. I made the basketball team in high school and did well, but I had to work very hard at it. The same thing was true with my studies: I had to work very hard. It became clear in retrospect, thinking about it, that, somewhere along the line, I got very clear messages that I was different from other people, that I was not as good as other people because of our poor "Okie" background. When you're from a poor background, working very hard and getting an education is the way up, the way to prove yourself. So I became very diligent. But that would never correct the inner void, the inner feelings of inadequacy. I later found that lots of people in A.A. felt a void or hole inside.

I never really got into trouble when I was growing up. There was tremendous reinforcement and support at home for my diligence, except when my mother was sick. If she felt well, both of my parents were at every sporting event I was in.

My mother became a private duty nurse, because it was easier than hospital work. She worked hard, seven days a week when she could. My parents' unspoken life plan revolved around her illness and impending death. They were working so hard to save money, because they were afraid she would die and there wouldn't be enough money for me to go to college. As close as I was to my mother, we never talked about it. That's only what I gathered at the time and pieced together since.

It turned out that she lived until I was sixteen. The aura of death, the unspoken but very palpable planning for death, lasted twelve years.

The medical advances now are such that if you get a disease like Hodgkin's today, you get treatment and you live. The difficult part [of knowing that] is, I don't have my parents. My life turned out okay, but I don't have my parents. Things could have been better.

I lost my dad when I was twenty, really from grief over my mother. There were complicating factors: My father didn't drink during the week, but after my mother died, he drank habitually on the weekends. He died of ulcerative colitis and liver failure. I think his escalated drinking was precipitated by my mother's death. It was a pretty dysfunctional time, personally, between the ages of sixteen and twenty.

I miss having my parents. It's kind of like, when you see other people who have kids, and you don't have kids. You're feeling happy for them, but you know you have a feeling of despair, too. I feel that way about people having parents.

My wife's parents are still alive. I'm the most involved with my father-in-law. When we get together, I hang out with him. He really likes me, because I pay so much attention to him. I like him, and I feel good about being with him, but the good gets mixed with remorse.

I still have very vivid dreams about my parents. My mom died in 1956 and my dad in 1960. I'll still wake up after having this long and detailed conversation with them. In my dreams, they look just like they did when they died. I'll wake up and say, "Now, that couldn't have happened; they died," but my subconscious knows no time frame. Part of me thinks I am, somehow or another, making contact with them or making amends, because my drinking really started and escalated just before my mother died and really got out of control after she died. I definitely have some guilt and remorse about "going off the deep end" between my mother's death and my dad's.

During those years, my drug of choice was alcohol. I had never heard of marijuana. From my first drink, I drank what I now know to be alcoholically, and got drunk. I did it over and over again. I'd be in a blackout and almost crack up the car. It's amazing that I survived my teen years. I wouldn't drink for awhile, and then there would be situations where I drank and got drunk. I drank and acted differently than other people. You hear about the "silent drinker" in A.A. Well, I wasn't like that. I was a danger on the streets when I got drunk, although I was always able to hold it together for my studies.

Everyone on the street knew when I was drunk and, somehow, I knew there was a real danger when I drank. Maybe that's why I didn't drink every day. When I was in medical school and graduate school at the same time (getting extra training), my personal life seemed to career. I'd have a relationship that would break up; I'd go on to the next relationship, and that would break up. I was engaged once, but she had very wealthy parents, and I had feelings of inadequacy, even though they seemed to like me a lot. I ultimately broke off the engagement.

I hit bottom (as an alcoholic) soon after that. I met this woman whom I thought I was in love with, whatever that was at the time. We had become sexual right away, and she'd gotten pregnant. She had seen me getting pretty crazy when I drank, and I was trying to convince her that I was stable. I wanted to marry her and be a father to the baby. She wasn't so sure; hence, the campaign to convince her I could be stable. In the middle of that, we went to a New Year's Eve party at which I got roaring drunk and ended up with another woman. The guy that the other woman was with threatened to shoot me. I had left the woman I was with (whom I loved and was trying to prove my reliability to), and, drunk out of my mind, I had taken this other woman out into a car. It was a total disaster. The woman I loved broke up with me, and went and had an abortion soon after. When I found out, I was very upset. That was really my alcohol bottom.

I really didn't drink again. That was January, 1966. I went to my first A.A. meeting around then, and I also went to Synanon. That was the big thing back then. It was also the beginning of the psychedelic period, and I smoked marijuana for the first time then. Marijuana won out over A.A. and Synanon. I really liked marijuana because I liked the way it made me feel. The really frightening thing about alcohol was losing control, but I didn't feel that I lost control with marijuana.

70

Not too long after trying marijuana, I took LSD, had a spiritual experience, and got into the work I'm in now. I had been aimed at academia—that was my career goal. I never in a million years thought I'd be in public health. I wanted to be a success, and an academic position along with a private practice of wealthy people (which would come from a prestigious academic position) was what I had in mind.

I became very interested in psychedelics. At the time, I explained my interest as "strictly academic." In addition, I happened to be living in an area where people were doing those drugs a lot. I'd be studying in the lab and seeing people doing them on the street as I walked home. You must understand, this was the time when LSD was acceptable in many academic circles. It was being seen as the breakthrough drug with all this potential. I took LSD, and the walls would dissolve, and all that. I interpreted that as a spiritual experience. I really never had a bad trip, but I liked marijuana better. Gradually I stopped doing LSD and did more marijuana.

In the late sixties and early seventies, after I had been smoking marijuana for a couple of years, my use escalated from occasional to nightly. I had marijuana in the psychedelic, spiritual context of the times at first; then it moved into a recreational context, except when I saw it as helping me go to sleep at the end of the day. I saw that as a separate issue.

Somewhere in those years, I got married. We had two girls. Despite smoking marijuana every day, my career was advancing. Over time, my wife and I grew apart in ways that were obvious to both of us. While the marriage was breaking up, I started developing a personal relationship with a woman who was totally drug free. To her, recovery meant no use of mood-altering substances. At the time, I was seeing all these people who were using drugs and dying, on the one hand, and all these people who had used and were living, on the other. I asked myself, "What was the difference?" Those who were living were going to Twelve Step meetings, and I thought maybe there was something there.

I had a working knowledge of Twelve Step programs from my professional work, but I really didn't endorse it, nor was I personally committed to it. The new woman in my life was into it; she challenged all that 1960's mentality of drugs being what people did to bring them closer to other people. That was my mentality. When we started living together, she said, "No drugs," and I interpreted it as "No drugs in the house."

I would go down to this friend's house, and as it turned out, he was a cocaine dealer, although I didn't know it at the time. I would go over to this guy's house to smoke. Since he was living in an apartment in a building I owned, I'd go there under the auspices of getting his rent money, but I always came back empty-handed and stoned.

I stayed away from the so-called addictive drugs because I knew I was addictive prone. I tried cocaine once and totally lost control. A lot of athletic injuries and surgeries along the way had introduced me to painkillers, and I loved the painkillers they'd give me. I always saw marijuana as a good drug and the others as bad drugs. I even read up on the latest research, so I considered myself quite knowledgeable about marijuana's safety. I didn't know that marijuana was incredibly subtle and capable of blindsiding the user.

After my wife and I had been living together for awhile, I dabbled in Twelve Step programs and thought I was in recovery because I wasn't drinking any more. Clearly, alcohol had been my *only* problem—or so I thought.

My marijuana bottom? I had come home after visiting that "friend of mine" one day. I put the joint out in my briefcase in a little can I always carried, but it didn't go out completely. This guy, this so-called friend, had just threatened to kill me if I evicted him. Mind you, I still had a romantic view of the drug culture, of people looking out for each other. Now I know it was all a justification for continuing to use, and for having a so-called safe place away from home to do it. The drug culture had turned rotten, and I had been trying to live in the 1960's drug scene mentality. I was thinking about all that as I came home, the remains of the joint I had just smoked smoldering in my briefcase. My seven-year-old daughter smelled it, and said, "Dad, you broke the family rule of no drugs." I had always preached "No drugs" to her, and she had caught me in all my hypocrisy. It was a very uncomfortable evening for all of us; my wife did an impromptu family intervention.

I woke up in the middle of the night with the words "half measures will avail us nothing" going over and over in my head. It was both a bottoming out and a spiritual experience at once. That night was a little like my first LSD experience in that it changed my life then, when I realized I had been doing half measures.[1] Thank God, I stopped there and got into recovery.

A good friend of mine had gotten busted a month before, for drunk driving, and he had made a commitment to A.A. So I called him the next morning and went to my first A.A. meeting, truly committed to the program. I said I

---

[1] In Chapter Five, "How It Works," of the *Big Book of Alcoholics Anonymous*, it says, "... half measures availed us nothing. We stood at the turning point. We asked His protection and care with complete abandon... Here are the steps we took, which are suggested as a program of recovery..."

was an alcoholic and a marijuana addict. I chose A.A. instead of Marijuana Anonymous or Narcotics Anonymous, because I needed a program that had the most spirituality and the most sobriety to counter my internal images of personal success, which had fueled my denial. Before I got into A.A., I remember times where I had interacted with old-timers (people who had many years in A.A.), and had felt like they had something I didn't have. I liked the old-timers in A.A. They had a program for living that I didn't have. The head stuff I had down pat; it was the soul stuff they had that I needed.

When I made a commitment to be in A.A., I went back to basics, got a sponsor, worked my Steps. I went to meetings where people wouldn't recognize me and ask me questions. I didn't want to be the public health expert as I was known in the area. I wanted to be an anonymous addict who needed help.

I've learned that marijuana really blocks your spiritual growth, and it blocks your ability to get into an A.A. program. I didn't get a strong Twelve Step program until I stopped using marijuana. When I stopped using marijuana, then I started to see how many areas marijuana had interfered with in my life, and how dependent I had become. For awhile, at the beginning, the urge to use left, but I would see situations when I would have used. For instance, when I traveled and felt isolated, I used to smoke a joint. Or I'd be working late, my mind would be going, and I'd smoke a joint to slow it down and sleep. Now, I choose to go out and find an A.A. meeting.

It took me a long time to clear. I think people who use don't realize their level of impairment. It's not dramatic, like alcohol; you don't black out, you don't go crazy, like with cocaine; but you don't realize how much marijuana takes over your life or impairs you until you stop. I'm referring to fuzzy mornings where you just can't be as responsive or productive as you can if you're not using. The thing I realized is, I'd always had trouble waking up. For years, I didn't do well in the morning. When I stopped, I realized a lot of my early morning impairment was, in fact, a cannabis hangover. I really didn't realize how much early morning impairment I had from smoking the night before, until a while after I had stopped.

Probably the most dangerous thing is how marijuana affects your judgment. Marijuana helped me sustain a belief in an era that no longer existed. For years, I had been sitting there, smoking marijuana with a cocaine dealer, thinking it was still the "summer of love." He was a liar and a cheat who could kill me. Hell, I was living in a twenty-year pot-induced time warp! For years, I had been putting my whole career in jeopardy, a career I had worked very hard to attain. And once I had attained it, I continued to work very hard maintaining it. Yet, on a daily basis, I had been running the risk of being busted for an illegal substance, going to jail, and ruining my professional reputation forever. I always had a case of joints in my briefcase.

People still stop me at conferences and ask to smoke a joint. I was always the one who had it. It was particularly dangerous during the period when I traveled with hair down to my shoulders, a marijuana tee shirt on, and a can of joints in my briefcase, going through airport security. I was like a red flag. At the time I felt, of course, "This is what you do." It wasn't until I was involved in the A.A. program that I realized how crazy that all was.

Maybe some of the marijuana advocates think they can use with no adverse effects, but I sure couldn't. And now I know my son sure can't. He experimented a couple of times last year when he was twelve, and it triggered a major depression for him. Just this week he was hospitalized, after having auditory hallucinations and a suicidal depression. They're finding that marijuana in young people can do this kind of thing. It's much more dangerous for adolescents, especially younger adolescents. Marijuana can precipitate psychotic episodes; we just don't know enough yet. There's this myth that marijuana's safe for people, but it sure as hell isn't safe for predisposed people.

For years, my second wife couldn't understand why I was still smoking. It used to drive her crazy that I was putting my career at risk, but when I was using, I couldn't see that. Here I was, a highly successful physician, well-known with a national reputation in my field, often lecturing throughout the world, only I had this secret.

What's it like now? My A.A. program has been beneficial and tremendously important to me. The spiritual program and the Twelve Steps have not only been an improvement for how to deal with life, but a way to deal with crises like I'm going through right now.The slogans, the Serenity Prayer, the support of people, the sharing, all contribute to my ongoing recovery and sobriety.

I think the first few years in recovery were spent in dealing with a lot of anger and resentment about what happened to me and anger at the drug culture. At first I experienced a lot of difficulty staying drug free and I had a lot of fear. The thing is, I'd wish I could have found the program without going through all that pain and misery. But the reality is, people don't find A.A. without going through misery and pain. That's where the phrase "grateful alcoholic" comes from. If they hadn't gone through all that pain and found the program, they wouldn't be so grateful. This is the most important thing in an addict's life.

Over time, it's easier to understand what people are saying in meetings. There are real physical advantages at first, but it takes awhile to get the spiritual and relationship advantages.

Several remarkable and tangible changes have occurred since I became sober. One in particular stands out. Every January I used to have an anniversary depression. That was the month my mother died, my father died, and my grandmother died. I'd always have this sense that bad things would happen in January. Since the second or third year of my A.A. program, my anniversary depression has gone away. I don't get upset for the month of January anymore.

I think the next step was having a spiritual program. Now I really appreciate the program and the value of *my program* with my family. It's a program for living, a guide for living, for how to deal with issues. At the beginning, you think that stopping the drugs is a big deal and, of course, it is, but the learning to live and deal with things differently is much bigger. When I have trouble falling asleep, I say the Serenity Prayer. I used to smoke a joint if something was bothering me. Now, if something's bothering me, I exercise, say the Serenity Prayer, pray. It used to be I didn't have a third way of dealing with things: I could either ruminate or get stoned. Now, I have a third way—my A.A. program. I call my sponsor. I work my program. A.A. has been a relief for me in my life.

I've worked the Steps. I'll give you an example: My heaviest drinking occurred in the years between my mother's and father's deaths. I didn't know how to make amends to dead people. People in A.A. gave me some suggestions. I went to my parents' graves with my aunt. She didn't understand what I was doing, but gave me the space. I said a prayer and talked to my parents.

My priorities have changed. The inner work, the spiritual work, seeing the January depression disappear—those are getting to be bigger and bigger rewards. Dealing with a particular issue and not relapsing—those are very important internal rewards. I also do a lot of A.A. service: driving people to meetings; picking them up. Most of the time, I don't speak at meetings, although I never refuse to speak when I'm asked. Recently, I went to speak at the International Doctors and Alcoholics Anonymous meetings, where there were around three hundred people in the audience. Afterwards, a couple of people came up and said, "That took a lot of courage for you to speak, because you're so well-known," I got a little anxious, because I hadn't thought of it like that. It had just been A.A. service to me, but as soon as I started thinking of the big picture—my reputation, my career—I got anxious. But I try to stay focused on my A.A. program and giving service—that's a very important part of my Twelve Step work.

I have been assured that this interview will be anonymous. I don't mind telling my story. Maybe it will help someone. The fact is that I am a well-known physician, who should have known better, but spent many years in denial, doing something that was a complete threat to my career, a complete threat to everything I had spent my life trying to accomplish. Fueled by my mother's beliefs that the way up was through education and becoming a doctor, I easily deluded myself into believing that I had to achieve at any cost. That is crazy, and hopefully my story will help other people see through their own denial.

The culture I came from said you had to do a drug to be an expert and talk about it. Look at Timothy Leary at Harvard…those were my times. If you understand your evolution and your recovery, you just have to accept that's the way it is. My history is part of my recovery. In fact, I thought I was in recovery because I didn't drink and I occasionally went to A.A. meetings. Now I believe you can't have a total commitment to recovery and experience spiritual growth unless you're drug free. I used to just read the Steps, but now that I know more, I actually work them.

It's interesting that I had less trouble with God than some people I've seen coming into the program after me. I think my early LSD experiences opened me up to spirituality. My sponsor says LSD is like a fast train to Paris, whereas A.A. is a much slower and more permanent trip. I take a very different view, now, of the interface between religion and spirituality. I always turned to God when disasters happened and said, "Why me?" and thought I'd done something wrong or I was being punished. I don't think like that anymore. That changed as I worked the program. I know half measures availed me nothing, and I have thought of that over and over many times.

My sponsor was crucial in helping me work my Steps. I still talk with him regularly. We work together on some projects and interact several times a week, and the interaction is a mixture of two relationships—professional and A.A. sponsor-sponsee.

I also carry a lot of A.A. tapes in my car and in my briefcase when I travel. I read the *Big Book*. It's really become integrated into my life. I particularly go over the early stuff from Bill Wilson (one of the founders of A.A.). I'm a real A.A. fundamentalist. I don't believe in modifying the program at all. I tried that for too long already, and found out the hard way, it doesn't work.

I think my wife and I are more on the same page these days. There have been very important improvements in our interactions. She has seventeen years in recovery, and I have six. We go to A.A. and get advice and help on things. We share the program. It's added a very important dimension to our relationship by giving us a common basis (in addition to our therapy) on how to deal with life. Most of our friends are in A.A. It's become an important part of our social life.

Our children have been exposed to Alateen and A.A. Unfortunately, some of it has backfired, because our son says, "You two had trouble, but came out of it okay."

After six years in the program, I can't say that what happens in life is always better, but how I deal with it is. I'm better about not ruminating, not getting down, not trashing myself during a crisis. I do depend on what the program teaches me. When I go to meetings, I try to be there early, stay after, talk with people, and do the whole ritual. I really look forward to it. When I first started going, I couldn't wait for the meeting to be over so I could leave, having "done it." But now, meetings are so important, I want to be there.

CHAPTER SEVEN
Grant

Age 56
Writer
Six Years of Sobriety

I'm fifty-six years old. During my childhood and early adolescence, although you didn't really hear too much about marijuana, what you did hear was pretty negative. It was definitely considered to be an immediately damaging drug. The prevention efforts at the time were based on the extreme spirit portrayed in the movie *Reefer Madness*. There was an hysterical fear of marijuana in the general public. I remember occasional references at home to people using marijuana. My parents' attitude, when they heard about a Hollywood star doing drugs or getting arrested, was that they were stupid or crazy for doing that. I subscribed to my parents' attitudes, which tended to be pretty conservative.

I guess a little background on my own sense of things would be useful. I was born and spent my first few years in Connecticut, close to New York City, and then came back when I was in the sixth grade. We spent those intervening years (1939-1948) moving on the average of two to three times a year, and that meant lots of different schools for me. My parents were older; they were both thirty-seven when I was born. I was around adults a lot and, as a result, I was a very adult-like child. I didn't ride a bicycle. I didn't climb trees. I had imaginary playmates I talked to, because I often spent long periods of time when there was nobody around. I was an inquisitive child. I was very interested in my surroundings, science, and the arts. I read very early! I didn't discover fiction until I was about eleven or so. Mostly, I read scientific books: astronomy, paleontology, archeology. I had projects and activities going all the time.

Shortly after we returned to Connecticut my father was diagnosed with bone marrow cancer. He got progressively sicker over the next five years. He was becoming less and less aware of what was going on. I was going into the throes of depression as my father was getting sicker. I also think my moods were urged on by my alcohol use. I got into alcohol pretty young, drinking in the eighth grade. We had a well-stocked liquor cabinet. I got very good at drinking what I wanted and filling up the bottles with water. My mother was pretty much a teetotaler and if she did drink, she always had mixed drinks, so she wouldn't have noticed the watered-down liquor.

As my father cycled in and out of the hospital for radiation treatments, I found myself feeling relieved when he went in and annoyed when he came out. Living in a house with someone with progressive cancer is very difficult. I think it is especially hard for a teenager. My dad was often irrational as his physical symptoms became worse. He smelled bad, and lost control over various faculties and bodily functions. His room smelled. I really had problems with it. At the same time I felt a lot of guilt for feeling angry, and then anger for feeling guilty, and I developed a decreased sense of self-esteem from it all.

In a few years, I saw him go from a dynamic, strong man to a walking skeleton. This was during the time I was twelve or thirteen to sixteen. It was very hard for my mom. She went through a period of sort of losing it right after Dad died. I had to step in and deal with things, which I felt totally inadequate to do. I checked into his military record, his burial set-up, questions about his pension, questions about medical bills, all that stuff a parent usually does.

Throughout that time I discovered that I had a tremendous capacity for alcohol, and alcohol provided me with a release from being an adult. I was able to capture the freedom of being a kid for the first time when I was intoxicated. Plus, that sort of plunged me into a very tightly-knit group of kids in my school. Even though I was finally settled into someplace, initially I didn't fit in anywhere. However, I could outdrink my schoolmates. Drinking gave me a reputation; it gave me a group of friends and an identity I was proud of. When I look back in my high school yearbook, half the notations from other kids were about drinking.

I graduated from high school in 1955. At that point, I had developed a pretty good identity. I excelled in sports by then. I had a reputation as a winner. I swam in competition. I had broken a couple of state records. I had been in Olympic tryouts. I had gotten into a pattern in high school where, during training and swim season I'd quit drinking and smoking cigarettes (which I had started doing at twelve in the Boy Scouts). But at the last swim meet of the year, I'd have a pack of cigarettes in my locker, and I'd light up after my last event. Talk about control ...

In any event, when I graduated from high school, I hung out with a small group of friends who enjoyed going down to Greenwich Village in Manhattan because we were enamored with the Bohemian spirit there. We were able to hang out and get served in the bars without an ID. I had grown a goatee at seventeen, and I called it my homegrown ID card.

I got to know a lot of the local folk over there, up-and-coming artists and writers, and they got mixed in with the parties we were having as teenagers close by in Connecticut.

Several of them smoked grass. I had heard about it, but had never seen it. One of them was a DJ for a local radio station. He was a very colorful kind of person whom somebody of seventeen, gravitating towards the Bohemian lifestyle, would really look up to. I had been thinking about marijuana, wondering what I would ever do if I was in a position of being confronted by it. For the most part, I had taken an anti-drug stand, but I wondered.

During that summer, I was a lifeguard. I had gone from being an ugly duckling to being a tanned, muscular guy in a relatively short time. I can't say that I regret that period too much. Anyway, I remember being at a party and going outside with a small circle of guys, and this DJ was teaching us how to smoke pot. He handed me the joint. The thought crossed my mind, "Well, I always wondered what I'd do if I was confronted with it," and I took a deep hit on it. That was my first experience with marijuana.

All three of us compared notes on our first experience over the next few days. We were very worried about it. We were all exposed to the prevention information of the times, which stated, "If you smoke marijuana once, you're morally down the drain forever." So, we went back three days later and talked to the DJ. "Hey, is there anything to all this stuff we hear about marijuana being addictive?" we asked him. He looked at us scornfully and said, "Look, I've been smoking reefer almost daily for fifteen years, and I have yet to see a sign of addiction." We wanted reassurance that it was okay. It had been great to take the initial risk, but God forbid we should do anything that would hurt us. We took our friend's statement as a go-ahead. Of course, now I interpret his statement very differently, but then it was *carte blanche* for us.

My mother had finally gotten through her grief process, and she had a new boyfriend with whom she was spending a lot of time, so I was pretty much left to my own devices. I had my own car. I had what amounted to, at my age, a very good income. It was both a happy and a sad time in my life. I felt depressed and alive. I didn't know what to do with my life. There were elements of chaos, aimlessness, and going nowhere fast [that were] counterbalancing the fun, high times we were having. Whenever we could, we smoked marijuana, but alcohol was more available to us, so we drank more often than we smoked.

In the fall, most of the time I went to school, but I just didn't go to classes. I went and played cards and talked to people. I had terrible grades. I was bored, as I had always been in school. What I read on my own had nothing to do with what they tested you on in school. I was writing a great deal. I was much more interested in what I was doing than what they were doing. Only once, in fourth grade, had school seemed worthwhile. My teacher discovered I was writing in class, and we struck a deal. Whenever I was beyond what they were doing, I could use that time to write (I was writing a novel) and, in exchange, once a week I'd get to read excerpts of my writing, and I'd get feedback. It was really great! It was the high point of my formal education. At community college I remained very unmotivated as far as school was concerned. I got out after two years and joined the Air Force.

When I went into the Air Force, I smoked when I came home on weekends and occasionally at parties. I wasn't smoking chronically until the end of 1959, when I came out of the military. That was the beginning of the Beatnik explosion; Kerouac had written *On The Road*, and Ginsberg's poetry had come out. I began hanging out in the Village again. I was writing this massive autobiographical novel along the lines of Dostoyevsky. I'd read chunks to anyone who'd listen. I worked on that novel for four years. I also spent those years trying to break into newspaper writing, but it was the middle of the Eisenhower Depression. I went in and out of schlock jobs; I smoked more pot, drank more, and really started to get into the experience of smoking.

In 1961 when I was about twenty-three, I went to visit some friends and met some very crazy people—early hippies. A writer down there was smoking pipefuls of *kif* (African pot). He came back with me. As we drove, we smoked pipefuls of that stuff. I got gloriously loaded. I think it was the first time I had potent enough stuff to really get the full effects of it. After that, I started shifting from "If it was there I smoked it," to seeking out marijuana to smoke. There was a lot of variation in quality, but it was becoming more important to me.

The hippie drug scene was starting. I think my alcoholism peaked. I got into a downward spiral. I couldn't hold down a job. Finally a friend and I started a landscaping business, but my partner decided I was too much of a rummy (which was funny, since we were drinking buddies) and bought me out.

Around that time I met Cynthia. She had been a student at City College in New York and had dropped out. She was sharing an apartment with three beauticians, not at all her type. The first time she saw my apartment, which was fairly large, she said, "Hey, can I move in with you?" I was living with another couple and feeling outnumbered, so I said, "Sure." Two days later she moved in.

Cynthia had been a fairly heavy marijuana smoker, and when she moved in, I started smoking marijuana more and drinking alcohol less. We became pretty much daily smokers. Maybe there were times we'd go several weeks, but I usually got access to very good dope. Friends would come over and we'd smoke and talk politics. Then about the time I was trying to get out of the relationship, our son was conceived. We tried raising money for an abortion without telling our parents. But we couldn't raise enough money so we decided, "What the hell, let's get married." The upshot was, we went down to Mexico, got married, and I went back to school.

Cynthia smoked marijuana all during her pregnancy. I was going to school on loans, scholarships, and the GI Bill. My drinking got into a binge pattern, where it stayed until I got into A.A. (twenty-five years later or so). Usually around the holidays I'd go into a major downward spiral for a few days, quit, try to control my drinking, then binge again.

Cynthia became a mommy. We knew there was something wrong with our son's behavior very quickly. Certainly, by the time he was four or five, we knew his behavior was often inappropriate. The way we dealt with it was to smoke pot every day and go away.

In graduate school, I began writing a massive experimental novel. I'd get up with the kids (by then we had a daughter, also), feed them breakfast, get them playing, and then I'd work on my book. I always had a hash pipe next to the typewriter and, throughout the morning, I'd load up the pipe and get progressively more stoned. My novel became progressively more complex and bizarre. Cynthia would get up around noon. We'd have lunch, go for a walk, come back, get stoned together, and pretty much go through the evening like that except when I had to go to classes or teach;

then I'd leave and take pot with me. By then, I was convinced I needed to change my consciousness every day. I was, as Grace Slick used to say, "Feeding my head." Things seemed flat if I didn't.

In the summer of 1966, we took LSD for the first time, and that was a major change! Suddenly I was a dedicated hippie. I had been interested in Eastern philosophies and religion and had read a lot about them. When I got into LSD, a lot of more-or-less legitimate research was being done on acid. I had been reading about Timothy Leary's research at Harvard and been very interested in trying LSD. A guy who worked at a local bookstore guided us through our first trip. We took LSD several times during that summer. I remember going back to school that fall and being another person. I felt like I had now experienced a lot of mystical stuff I had read about. LSD always scared the daylights out of me, but I liked the results so much, I kept doing it. I felt I owed it to myself as a writer to explore different consciousnesses.

By then, smoking grass daily was a way of life. My pattern was: I'd get up early in the morning, smoke a joint on the way to school, teach a class, talk to my students, go smoke a joint, go to a class or two, go to a bar in town, drink, and then smoke pot on the way back. The pot smoking basically went on all through graduate school, where I was almost a straight A student. Actually, somewhere in there, just before Cynthia got pregnant with our daughter, I went through a traumatic alcohol binge where I lost my car keys and went sort of crazy for a couple of days, finally got home, and quit drinking alcohol completely for the next three years. But I was smoking grass every day. It seemed like the ideal drug. I could function behind it.

We emigrated to Europe right after I finished graduate school. That was the year Kent State happened (1970). I was convinced there was going to be a civil war along age lines in this country, and I wanted to get all four of us out. At this point in time, we were very mellow people on macrobiotic diets. My fantasy of becoming a stringer with an American newspaper didn't pan out and, within a couple of months, we came back, dead broke. We lived with some old friends in New Hampshire for awhile, and then moved out to California where we found some old friends living in a commune in Northern California. We lived nearby and got on welfare for a year, which really took its toll on us.

Cynthia and I were not doing well when we took an acid trip at the end of that year. It turned out to be the acid trip from hell. What was really weird was, before tripping I had cast the *I-Ching*, and it had said, "Blood dissolves." I was wondering what that meant. All our plans for a beautiful acid trip in the country went wrong. The field was being sprayed, we were being buzzed by a DEA (Drug Enforcement Agency) plane; it was horrible. In the middle of that, I admitted to Cynthia that I had started smoking cigarettes again. I think that was the straw that broke the camel's back. Cynthia went off, ranting and raving about me and the cigarettes. She packed up things, took the kids, and left. She ended up back at her parents' home in the Midwest. That *I-Ching* reading has stood out in my mind ever since.

I went out on about a three-week drunk. I thought I was dying. It seemed like the world had crashed down. Finally, I cleaned up and hitchhiked to Cynthia's parents' house. I stayed several months while we got back together.

We went back to California and moved to a commune. Shortly after, Cynthia met another man, and they moved to New Hampshire with the kids. I went through a lot of difficulty when that happened, doing a lot of psychedelics, and smoking grass every day to cope. I ended up staying on as the resident shaman and librarian for about a year and a half after that.

Towards the end of my stay in the commune, we were hosting a large wedding. People were coming from all the communes around. I realized a number of women I was dating were going to be in the same place at the same time, a potentially uncomfortable situation. I took a large amount of LSD so I wouldn't have to get involved. That day I met Virginia, and we started dating. She smoked marijuana, too, but not necessarily daily. We'd smoke it and stay pretty stoned when she'd come and visit. We ended up deciding to move down to Santa Cruz and live together. We were both out of work. I remember thinking one night in my tent at the commune, "What's going to happen when I go back?" And I realized there is no going back, only forward. It was a magical period.

It took me a year to find a steady job at a grassroots organization. I started out as a half-time janitor and secretary. I quickly worked my way up to being their main writer. I had stopped doing psychedelics. I was drinking on a long-wave binge cycle. I was pretty much a maintenance smoker, starting with my joint when I woke up, and pretty much smoking every few hours until my last joint before bed. I was becoming increasingly isolated.

I could pretty much do what I wanted on the job. We moved out of town to the country. Mornings, I would smoke a joint, take a walk, think about great book ideas, but basically get nothing done. I got away with it because the organization I was working for had such a nurturing, accepting atmosphere. That is, until we got a new director, who had all the right politics, but who happened to be drug free and in recovery. Of course, that didn't come out at first. I think she realized what was happening with me and quietly started bringing in a consciousness of recovery.

Right around that time, I had gotten a call from a publisher loosely affiliated with our organization, and he asked me to write a book about meditation and other methods of getting high on life naturally. I was thrilled. At first, I thought I could do it living as I had been living, but the more research I did, the more I realized I couldn't do the book justice if I was stoned as I was writing it.

Basically, when I started working seriously on the book in 1984, I quit everything. I didn't have a program; I just white-knuckled it. When I stopped smoking marijuana, I had the realization that I did not need to be chemically boosted on a daily basis. A week passed, and I was still alive. I wasn't climbing the walls; disaster hadn't struck. It wasn't that hard to stop. I began to realize I didn't need to be chemically boosted at all. It helped that I wasn't associating with anyone on a regular basis who was still smoking. On rare occasions I'd find myself in places where people were lighting up a joint, and I'd feel a desire to smoke like them, and I'd think, "No. No way!" Along the way I did a lot of research on the Twelve Step programs and how they worked, because they overlapped with many ideas in the book. I was white-knuckling it from 1984 until 1988. By the time I finished the book, I was convinced I'd never start again.

A few months later, when it was published, I said, "I'm pretty much convinced I'm an alcoholic, but I'm going to take one last shot at controlled drinking. If it doesn't work, I'll go to A.A. and play by the book." I started drinking again, and I went to some meetings as an observer. I began to realize that my attitude, that A.A. was composed of religious weirdos, was wrong. As I listened to people with long-term sobriety, I became more and more convinced that that was the direction to go. The people in N.A. also made sense to me. It was okay for about six months. Then my wife, Virginia, went off to a conference. I dropped her off at the airport at 11 A.M. and, by 11 P.M., I was in a drunk tank having a major First Step breakthrough. That's my A.A. birthday—March 8, 1988. Parenthetically, I realized the whole concept of controlled drinking was a contradiction in terms. It doesn't work.

The thing that I found with marijuana was that the full impact of it was not apparent to me when I was using. I hadn't noticed any lack of motivation or productivity, although the last few years I was getting the sense I should stop. When I'd smoke, I'd know, "This drug is giving me an overlay that everything is okay, but I know everything is not okay." I'd find myself smoking a joint and saying, "This isn't good for me; this is something I have to stop."

Through the years, I had smoked a lot of very strong marijuana, and I had extreme anxiety and paranoia. My heart would start racing, and I'd wonder if anyone ever died from this. But I also continued, despite these frequent experiences, to see it as an ally. Pot was the drug I lived; alcohol was the drug I used to act out. I lost a long period of time because of pot—a very long period of time.

It was a long process. It took me a few years to see the long-term effects. Though I thought I was very spiritual and involved in Eastern thought and meditation, I wasn't. I was only mystically involved. There's a difference. Spirituality involves interaction with a higher power and with manifestations of that higher power in your surroundings and with other people. Marijuana really cuts you off from all that. I could never have gotten into A.A. or recovery had I still been smoking pot.

It was pretty incredible, developing a sense of spirituality after realizing I was so cut off. I had been drug free for four years, but I was still toxic when I started going to A.A. I hadn't made that shift. In May, 1988, I went for a hot tub and massage. I was lying back in the tub looking up at the stars. I was fifty years old, in recovery for two months, and realizing that, in India, they divide life into four parts. The first twenty-five years are sort of going around raising hell. For the second twenty-five years, you're a householder and business person. The third twenty-five year period is for getting on a spiritual path. And the fourth is coming back and teaching. I had been wondering as I was approaching fifty, "What would a spiritual path look like in the West?" Lying back in the hot tub, I thought, "It's here! I'm there! It's happening!" I had this massive attack of bliss. A lot of spiritual things came together at that moment.

At the beginning of my recovery, I asked my director, the woman I had seen as a great threat to my using, to be my sponsor. She agreed to be my temporary sponsor, which gave me time to find the person who has been my sponsor ever since.

I've gotten a strong sense that when you're high, you replace your own ability to experience a variety of things by experiencing them through the drug. It took several years, and even now I occasionally find myself really appreciating again the intense level of experiencing life as it is without smoking marijuana, like really seeing the blue sky, the spring green grass.

I can feel a progressiveness. I went through some long bouts of depression in early recovery, but tried to be more aware and more in tune with my Higher Power during those times, and after. I'm realizing I won't find God's will by looking for esoteric signs. It's what's happening. I've needed to learn to let things change. The best way to deal with the changes is through my attitude.

My relationship with my wife Virginia has changed tremendously. We were on very shaky grounds before I quit, but we're not anymore. I've undergone some fairly extensive personality changes in the process of recovery, such as changing from black-and-white thinking to becoming a lot more flexible. One example: We were planning a trip to Europe, and Virginia had brought out that we like to go out to eat, and she suggested we eat fewer dinners out to save money for the trip. I, in turn, said, "Hey, in the summer neither one of us works, so we could go out for lunch instead of dinner; it's less expensive." My wife looked at me kind of funny and said, "You've really changed, because a few years ago, you'd have gone into a snit and said, 'Okay, we won't go out to dinner anymore! We'll just save money for the trip.'"

There are still scars, and a lot of lost time and abraised feelings. Those may never heal completely. I've found I have to accept that and deal with it a day at a time. It's worth it, because this is progressive. What there is now is so much better than what there was.

I used to get creative ideas, but they'd go up in smoke. In all the years I was smoking (and seeing myself as a creative writer), there was an occasional article, a newsletter, and one book. I'd written other things but never finished them, or if I finished them, I never followed through to publication with them. In the eight years since I quit smoking pot, I've published nine books, and I'm working on three more right now.

In looking back, I think one of the things that got me into using was this weird cultural veneration for the aberrations of creative people. When I was in college, my mentor would say things like, "Wordsworth was a very good wordsmith, but his one problem was that he was too normal." There's a sort of veneration of the suffering, tormented, stoned artist. And I bought that. What I tell people now when I'm teaching is, "We've had some giants who managed to do very creative things despite their drug use, but God knows what they would have done without their drug use."

Life is so much fuller now! After six years in recovery, I'm still getting insights into what I did to myself (and other people I loved) when I was using, and how negative those times really were. And to think I was convinced of marijuana's innocence.

CHAPTER EIGHT
Alicia

Age 45
Mother and Independent Film Editor
Eight Years of Sobriety

I was the third-born child in our family, the first girl. My birth was very difficult, and I was born with multiple physical problems. In fact, the doctors weren't sure what I'd be capable of doing in my life, and they warned my parents not to have very high expectations. I guess I was diagnosed with cerebral palsy and brain damage. It seems things were not in their correct places in my brain. My parents were very worried about me. They took me to an osteopath when I was only a few months old. He manipulated the bones of my skull in order to relieve pressure on my brain. My mother tells me I screamed agonized screams during these sessions. Amazingly, it worked, though I did continue to have some vision and coordination problems.

My mother had this thing about our family: we were "special," "better than" other people. Somehow that message separated us from other people. One of my brothers was only eighteen months older than I. Being so preoccupied about me, my mother neglected him. He quickly grew to hate and resent me. He was always doing his best to make things miserable for me as a child. I found myself at an early age trying to appease his wrath and make things okay for him. That kind of codependent pattern haunted me later in other relationships with moody men. For whatever reasons, I became a very sweet, naive child, despite getting teased by other kids a lot because I looked a little different. I didn't know how to protect myself from being hurt; I just knew how to be.

I grew up in an alcoholic home. Both my parents were alcoholic. They mostly drank in the evenings. While cooking, my mother would reach up into the cupboard and pour glass after glass of gin. Frequently, the food would be overcooked and her words would be slurred at dinner. When she drank, she adopted an arrogant, bossy attitude that was an even greater magnification of her normal assertiveness. My father suffered from depression a lot, going through days, perhaps nursing a hangover, torturing himself with existential issues, lashing out at whoever dared show exuberance near him. When he was drunk, he'd take on a playful, expansive personality. It was like Jekyll and Hyde. We all tiptoed around him, and my mother shielded him from us. She knew how to make him look good and cover up for him. And the veil of secrecy and being special was there to insulate us.

There ended up being six kids in our family—three girls and three boys. We lived in the South, not the Deep South, just the South. We were encouraged to participate in school. I was a really good student despite early medical predictions that I might be mentally retarded. I also ended up excelling at swimming, and that became important to me as a kid.

When it came time to go to college, I chose a nontraditional school in the Midwest. I was ready for something very different. At this school, you'd alternate between spending one quarter on campus studying and one quarter in a job placement. It was kind of hard to make and keep friends, because people were always rotating in and out. You learned to get to know people quickly. We had a pass/fail system after the first quarter, so it was pretty easy to get by.

About a month after I started college, a boy I liked invited me to his room to try smoking pot. He and his roommate were there. They had a little sawed-off pipe. When I smoked the pot, it was very harsh and hot. I coughed. Still, I gamely followed their instructions to hold it in, and I got high. Everything seemed distant and strange. Unfortunately, this boy decided this was a very good time to try kissing me for the first time. It was also my first kiss, ever. His lips felt like worms, and I felt unhappy and alienated. Despite this first not-so-great experience, I went on to try smoking in other circumstances, so there was obviously something about it that I had liked.

I was working on a lot of other stuff besides school at first—boys, drugs, the Vietnam War protests. Drugs were not my main focus that first quarter or two, although I certainly grew to enjoy them a lot. We'd smoke pot, sit around, have these philosophical talks, and laugh a lot. It was great feeling like I fit in and belonged, instead of that old family-instilled sense of being different, special, and separate. I felt a protection, a safety, a sameness in being high. Maybe that's why I liked pot so much; it felt like being in a safe cocoon.

Not long after I started smoking pot, I felt I had a problem with it, because I wanted to smoke it a lot and sought out people who had it. I would go and hang around until I got invited to share some. Even though I enjoyed most of the times I was smoking with people, and hadn't started smoking alone, I felt there was something wrong about my attraction to it and my growing obsession with it. I went to my faculty advisor and talked to him about it. I cried. He seemed to think it would be easy to steer away from it by pursuing other interests, such as drama. Even as he gave me his good advice, I felt an undercurrent of hopelessness about the power the drug had over me. Nothing seemed as attractive as getting stoned.

That next summer, in between my first and second years in college, I went to Mexico. I knew Spanish and thought I'd major in language. I enjoyed Mexico, but noticed I really missed pot. I was still in a place where I wouldn't have risked smoking it down there, knowing the laws were really strict; instead, I tried smoking cigarettes, but it wasn't the same, so I stopped.

I had a boyfriend on campus before I left, and he didn't smoke pot. After Mexico, I went back to see him for a few weeks before going to South America. The other students and I lived with Colombian families. My boundaries were still pretty clear about what was dangerous, but we did manage to get stoned at other Colombian students' apartments, never at the family's home. That was real pot—a lot stronger than what I was used to.

I met another woman student from the Midwest, and we became fast friends. I remember we both enjoyed the details we'd notice and the word games we'd play when we were stoned. The two of us became friends with a Colombian artist. I began to like him more and more and we became close friends.

During that time, my American boyfriend stopped answering my letters. I wrote quite a few times before finding out from my brother (the one born right after me who was at the same school) that he had a new girlfriend. I was heartbroken and cried for days. I think that set up a pattern for me: I believed if I was naive and sensitive, always giving people the benefit of the doubt, then they'd walk all over me and break my heart. I needed some protection, and pot came to the rescue.

Soon after that, my Colombian artist friend and I became lovers. I felt completely justified being stoned all the time with him. We communicated better, and I couldn't be hurt because I wasn't really that involved. The pot kept me one step removed, in my cocoon. I didn't feel vulnerable when I was high.

After that quarter, my friend (the woman from the Midwest) and I decided to stay on in Colombia and teach English. I had just turned twenty. We'd teach seven to nine classes a day. We got our own apartment. We weren't very good at taking care of ourselves. I think we practically lived on French toast and hard-boiled eggs. We partied every night, smoking a lot of pot. It was so cheap! I started smoking in the morning before teaching. I noticed my roommate looking at me kind of funny when I did that. I had a great rationale: smoking pot made it easier to get onto the crowded bus where we were like sardines. We'd often get touched and not know who was touching us. It was not fun, but being high gave me some distance. The only problem was, midway through the morning, I'd crash. I wanted to go to the bathroom and get stoned, but I was scared, and wouldn't.

At night we'd just get stoned and more stoned. At the end of the second quarter in Colombia, my friend and I thought about staying, but decided not to. I had an inkling that something was wrong with my life and with how I smoked pot. I saw going back as a positive move. However, I was able to justify smuggling six ounces of pot in my underwear and another wrapped in my long hair. My friend did the same. We were both so nervous going through customs, but we also had a sense of infallibility. She and I went our separate ways after that.

I went back to campus and sold some of the pot. I was impressed with how much I could get for it. I started occasionally going to class stoned that quarter. I had the idea it enhanced class and helped me make clever observations, but sometimes, I'd be halfway through and forget the clever observation I was making.

Somehow I started smoking alone more often. I had a sense that I needed my pot-induced cocoon for protection, but I think I also knew at the time, or maybe it was just later in retrospect, that my cocoon was hardening and becoming more like a shell. A powerful image from that time is: I'm sitting by an open window. It's forty degrees below zero outside. I'm smoking pot and blowing the smoke out the window so my housemates won't think I smoke too much.

By my senior year, I was getting stoned in the mornings. I was an assistant teacher on the East Coast the first quarter. I'd have to take the subway to school, but sometimes I'd get so depressed and freaked out on the way that I'd turn around, go home, and get stoned all day. When I did go in, the teacher wouldn't give me anything to do, so I'd be bored. It should have been a great job, but it was horrible.

When I went back to college, I fell for another guy. He didn't smoke pot, so I guess I cut back when I was spending a lot of time with him. It was actually pretty good for me not to be smoking pot so much. We were living with people who weren't into it. I reconnected with people. By the second quarter, the relationship wasn't going so well, and he moved out. I spent the rest of my senior year obsessing about getting him back.

My brother and I didn't have a lot to do with each other at school. He did pot, too, but mostly he drank. When we went home to see our family, it was different. We'd get stoned together a lot. He and I "turned on" our younger brothers and sisters.

I smoked pot all the time when I was home. There was this underlying history with so many unresolved feelings— you know, those issues you're supposed to deal with in your late teens and twenties, like separating from your family, codependence with your father, anger with your mother. But I didn't know at the time I was supposed to be dealing with them. I was basically not growing up; I was not dealing with any of that. All I knew was I didn't feel comfortable there, and pot made me feel not so uncomfortable, so I smoked it.

I turned a corner in my pot smoking when I graduated from college. I didn't know what to do. My mother lined up a job for me in my hometown. I went back to smoking pot every day. I lived in a small apartment complex my parents owned, and managed the place in exchange for rent. I rode my bike six miles to and from work every day that summer. All I remember from that time was not wanting to feel sad, lonely, or hurt, so I smoked pot. At lunch, I'd take a walk in a nearby park and get stoned. Once my supervisor asked why my eyes were so red when I came back, and I think I discovered Visine around then. That was kind of an isolating summer.

At the end of the summer, I decided to go back to college, hang out, and audit classes. I also tried to get my old boyfriend interested in me again, but that didn't work. I smoked a lot of pot, did half-assed jobs like cleaning houses, lifeguarding—I didn't really know what to do. By March, I knew going back hadn't been such a good idea. I went home again to wait for replies from my graduate school applications. A few days after I got home, someone I had known in college called me about a job in Los Angeles. Instead of pursuing graduate school, I went to L.A. I thought a geographic change might help.

I continued smoking a lot of pot every day in L.A. From 1971 on, I pretty much smoked every day until beginning recovery in 1986. I'm talking, like, probably mornings before going into work, one joint at noon, one as soon as I got home, and one more in the evening—easily four or five joints a day.

Good things started happening for me in L.A. I was in a women's group. We'd sit around, smoke pot, and talk for hours. I felt connected. Smoking was once again social and fun. I met my future husband, Jonathan, in 1973. He liked alcohol, and I started drinking regularly with him.

Work was difficult. I was videotaping family therapy sessions from behind a one-way mirror. I'd be watching all this pain. I couldn't stand being that close to that much pain, and so I "needed" the pot to distance myself. The drawback? I'd screw up scheduling and other detail work. It became a game to see how high I could get and still look like I was in control on the job. It was like a contest between the drug and me.

In 1976, after five years on the job, I quit and went down to South America with a woman friend. This story shows how my lines of danger had changed over time. I took a little pot with me, and after it was all used up, I wanted more. I scored and smoked pot in the Amazon, even though it was dangerous. Our two boyfriends met us in Bogota. We were all in a park, she and I were smoking, and a policeman started approaching us. We put out the joint. He came over and said, "Empty your pockets." We had a roach left. When he said "You're coming with me," my traveling companion said, "Sir, is there something we can pay as a fine?" He ended up taking $30 and walked away. We could have all been in prison for years. I had jeopardized all our lives by smoking there. That was one of those times when reality intruded and said, "You're taking some ridiculous risks here," but I kept going.

There's another important story during that trip to South America. I was growing pot in L.A. I had eight or ten huge plants growing in the backyard. I even had a rabbit, because they said rabbit poop was really good fertilizer for pot. Anyway, Jonathan was in the shower when a policeman, his gun drawn, knocked at the door. He had gotten a call that there had been a shooting at the house. He came in and looked around, but didn't see the pot plants. If he had, Jonathan would have been taken to jail. We never knew who placed that call, or if it was a wrong address or what. Yet despite both those incidents, Jonathan didn't say anything about my pot smoking. And after the plants were harvested, he never said anything about my selling it.

I didn't do a good job selling it. I was supposed to sell a pound to this one guy. I didn't have a scale, so I tied a loaf of bread to one end of a yardstick and tried to use that as a scale. The guy called, really angry that it was a couple of ounces low. I gave him more. A few days later, the rest was stolen from our house; nothing else was taken. I was so angry! I wanted to go to the police, but I couldn't. That guy was murdered eight years later.

I got a new job at a foreign-speaking television station when I returned to the states. I began hiding my pot smoking from Jonathan by going on walks and getting stoned away from him, or smoking in the bathroom, even though he wasn't saying anything. At work one day after I had been smoking in the bathroom, a coworker said, "I smelled pot in the bathroom this morning." I replied by asking, "Who would do that?"

My contest continued: "How stoned could I get and still make this edit?" I also used pot as a sedative to deal with stress at work. If I went half a day and didn't smoke, I'd get irritable.

We moved up to the Northern Coast area in 1979. I had a sister up there who became my smoking buddy. By then, sinsemilla (locally-grown, extremely strong pot) was on the scene. She and I grew some inside, with lights and all. When we moved from there, we decided to stop growing it and, again, my judgment was crazy. She and I loaded all the plants and equipment into an old van and drove it across town. It stalled on the way. We could have been busted. We gave it all to a friend. A few days later, my sister had regrets and we went to get it back. That was crazy—people kill over things like that—but the two of us went over there, argued with the guy, and left with all the stuff.

Jonathan and I had been trying to have kids up there, and I was smoking sinsemilla all the time. It was very painful, not getting pregnant. I was dealing with infertility, and how did I deal with it? I'd smoke more pot. There was this guy where I was working who was the biggest pothead I'd ever seen. He'd smoke and sell it from his back office. This was that skunkish smelling pot. Man, was it ever strong, stronger than the sinsemilla, and I got into it! We'd smoke it throughout the day. That's when I really felt a craving for it. I just wanted to go smoke the stuff, because I liked the way it made me feel. My job involved a lot of math, logic, short-term memory, details. I knew smoking pot made it harder for me to work, so I decided to quit that job. My rationale was, maybe with less stress I'd be able to get pregnant. Looking back, I realize it was really the amotivational syndrome, but I didn't know it at the time.

I could barely function on the new pot I was smoking. I got a new job that was much easier and less stressful, but I had to wear an alarm watch so I'd remember to do the things I had to do. Sometimes the alarm went off and I didn't remember what it was set for. I'd have to rehearse what I was supposed to do to keep it straight. The game I used to play in L.A. came back, but with an added element, which I later realized was my mother's old message: I was going to overcome this problem because I was special. I had overcome my early handicaps; I could certainly outwit pot. I was different, special, and separate with my secrets. I was living out those old prophecies and they were killing me. Lord knows what I could have done if I hadn't been a pothead. But I'm getting ahead of myself. At the time, my conscious rationale was that the job was so easy, if I got stoned I could make it harder and more of a challenge.

We finally adopted a child. I switched to working weekends so I could take care of Paul during the week, and Jonathan could take care of him on the weekends. I was home alone with Paul five days a week. My drug habits changed. I only smoked pot while he napped and when we went for walks, but I began drinking more at night.

Paul was a very irritable baby. It seemed like if I smoked, I could distance myself from his feelings. Slowly I started smoking more. Over time, that began backfiring. I didn't have a sense of my feelings until they got really strong, and then I'd erupt. When I did, my outbursts would startle both of us. My rationale for smoking at that point was that when I was stoned, I'd be really playful with him. So there were still some positive things going on.

My pot smoking also began to take its toll on my relationship with Jonathan. When I'd start coming down and feel so rotten, I'd blame it all on Jonathan. The cocoon from pot was really keeping us apart.

Then I discovered that if I drank quite a bit of alcohol and then smoked pot, it would control the degree to which I felt drunk. I thought it was a nice combination. I pushed us to drink more.

We moved to the Bay Area in 1982. I didn't know anybody. Through my job I found someone to buy pot from. It was $200 an ounce. I started smoking from a pipe so I wouldn't waste as much. Cocaine was big, too. I tried it but, thank God, it made me real nervous, so I didn't do it again.

I noticed I was having a lot of lung problems. I had been coughing before, but in the Bay Area, I was coughing in the morning, in the evening, and after a bowlful. I sounded like I had emphysema, wheezing and coughing. Soon it seemed like I was coughing all the time. Finally, Jonathan started asking why I had to smoke or drink so much. It was a year before I got into recovery, and could answer his question truthfully, "Because I can't stop."

About two years after we moved to the Bay Area, when our first child was three, we adopted our second child. I was stoned all the way through that adoption process. I even smoked on the way to the hospital to pick her up when she was born. I was smoking throughout the day, no longer waiting for naps. I feel really sad about that now.

Jonathan and I were having more relationship problems, and I started having trouble sleeping. I didn't know it was from the alcohol I was drinking. I went to see our general practitioner and told him I was tired all the time. He told me that was because I had two little kids. I told him I was also smoking pot and drinking a lot. He gave me the twenty-item assessment test on alcoholism and told me to see if I could go a week without using. I couldn't, but thought it was because it had been a "special" week with lots of extra things going on. I told him not to worry; I'd work it out.

A year later, I found myself back in his office. He said I should go into an inpatient program. I reminded him that I had two little kids and couldn't possibly go into an inpatient program. He said, "So, go to the outpatient program." I left the doctor's office and went straight over to the outpatient office and said, "I have to do something; I have to stop; my husband is going on a business trip." I knew I couldn't handle the household without Jonathan for a week. I think it was a combination of not sleeping, coughing all the time, and bringing up kids in that environment. I also knew I was down to my last bud. I had to stop without any in the house and before buying more.

They took me right away. I started that evening before I could change my mind. The most amazing thing happened about a week later. I had a flashback to twenty years before, when I had first gotten addicted; nothing in my life had really changed. I was that mental age, having to start over. It was twenty years later, and the twenty years were nothing! From that flashback, I realized I'd just blown all this time. I knew I had a lot to do, and I was afraid it would take another twenty years to catch up. I had all this regret! It was a very powerful realization and helped keep me in treatment.

I guess while I was in the intensive treatment program, I hid a lot by helping other group members. I worked really hard doing that. I tried to protect myself and feel "better than" by being the best at recovery and being able to help others. I could give, but I couldn't receive from other group members, although I did allow the counselor to help me. The counselor never seemed to call me on it, although my memory is probably not so clear from that time.

When I had been growing up, my family had no belief in God. They believed you had to rely on yourself. The messages we got about being so special resulted in all of us feeling omnipotent. We all had big cases of arrogance and terminal uniqueness. We also all thought we had to do it on our own, and had major control issues. But in recovery, they were telling me if I didn't develop a relationship with a higher power, I wouldn't be able to stay sober. I felt stuck. They told me to look for evidence that there was a God.

About two weeks into my recovery program, I got a call from a young cousin of mine, who told me that she and her boyfriend were having a baby and wondered if we would be interested in adopting the baby. I took that call as a spiritual experience, that there was a reason I had gotten into recovery when I had. Without recovery, there's no way I could have or should have had another child. I couldn't really contend with the two I had. Without a recovery program, there's no way I could have built a trusting relationship at that point in time. That whole set of circumstances helped me believe there was a power or a plan, and I didn't have it.

They ended up coming out for a week to get to know us more and see if they were comfortable with us adopting their baby. They were young, not ready to start a family, and my cousin didn't believe in abortions. I approached their visit differently than I had ever approached a stressful situation before: I used some tools from the program. I tried not to have expectations, and just let things work out, instead of having a controlled agenda. The week went well.

After they left, I got a phone call telling me my mother had inoperable cancer. The timing of that phone call showed me God doesn't give me more than I can handle. I was clean and sober, my cousin and her boyfriend were gone, the new baby issue was resolved, and here came another biggie to contend with. But I could deal with it. I knew I'd have tons of amends to make to my mother for not being there all those years, but I sensed that with help, I could do it. It ended up being as good an experience as losing your mother can be. Without the program, I would have been a stoned mess. With it, I was able to feel my feelings and learn from them.

Four months after the intensive outpatient program was over, a therapist friend of mine suggested I find a therapist to help me with the issues that kept flooding in. She said they usually don't recommend a therapist in the first year of recovery, but she knew one who specialized in chemical dependence. She reassured me that my issues were a natural residue from years of stuffing feelings, perceptions, and living life but not really dealing with it. I called the woman she suggested. That was the beginning of an important five-year relationship.

Our early work was about trust and staying sober. My therapist reminded me years later that I went in six-to-eight week cycles, where we'd be going along fine in our work, and then I'd spend a session or two in major questions and want to leave. I'd grapple with not trusting her and not believing it to be worth it. I'd be so scared, I'd twist what she said, wanting to make her bad so I could justify leaving therapy. The better our work was going, the more I wanted to run away. Sometimes I needed phone calls in between sessions to get me to come back, because I was so sure I had found a fatal flaw to prove I shouldn't be working with her.

My therapist said she tried to deal with each question, each allegation I brought up, but after my pattern persisted for over a year, she'd occasionally suggest maybe I should take a break and see, with some distance, if the work we were doing was valid. She didn't want me to feel coerced or forced into staying, which is what I sometimes accused her of doing. When she'd say that, I'd really be scared, because she was giving me the "out" I was looking for, but another part of me knew I couldn't take it. I also resented her because I felt stuck. Somehow we made it through. It took almost two years for me to really begin to trust her. I couldn't have done the stuff we did after that until I proved to myself that my fears weren't real.

When we talked about it later, I realized I was using her to test the idea of trusting significant people in my life, so all those struggles I went through, which at times were grueling for her and for me, paid off. Later, she told me that as long as I kept coming back and putting myself in her office, she knew at least part of me wanted to get healthy, and she tried talking to that part of me no matter how hidden or open it was. I guess she had faith in me long before I was able to have faith in me, in her, and in the therapeutic process.

My therapist was able to point out (until I got it) how I was "in my head" defending against my inner feelings (like I had in treatment). I had to learn how to overcome this ridiculous dichotomy. I'd flip between arrogance, assuming everything I did was perfect, and incredible insecurity about everything in my life. The arrogance and perfection were a defense to keep me going and look like I was doing well.

Right before I entered recovery, I had been despondent. I had no hope. I even had suicidal thoughts that would come and go. But within a few days of starting my recovery program, that was gone. Meetings were really good for me. Early on I heard an A.A. speaker who convinced me this was a disease. I could listen and be with my feelings. There's no cross-talk at meetings, so I wasn't obligated to show how well I was doing. I couldn't escape by giving advice to others. I developed a lot of humility sitting there, hearing people talk, and knowing how much I could relate. I admired how people operated in those rooms. I liked their sincerity and genuineness.

I had a lot of self-blame, and I was hyper. I had all this energy, and I didn't know what to do with it. I was very irritable and angry at first—dangerously so with the kids—and then I'd feel horribly guilty. I found that, without my sedative (pot) to rely on, I needed other things to deal with my extra energy. I took up lap swimming and did relaxation tapes.

I never felt stoned that whole first year, but I definitely felt crazy, as if I had emotions whipping around my body and being out of my control. My therapist helped me realize my worst times were due to PMS (premenstrual syndrome). I had a difficult time accepting that PMS was indeed a physical handicap; plus, I felt like I already had enough with a vision problem, early physical problems, and now the disease of chemical dependence. But once I stopped fighting the idea, I started trying different things that helped me with the symptoms.

That first year, between feeling that what I was learning in therapy and at meetings was helping, I'd feel out of control and angry. I just barely knew it would pass and I'd feel different if I didn't get stoned.

I continued to see how my early childhood stuff—my physical and visual problems—had set me apart from other kids. That reality and my mother's insistence that I was special in a wonderful way didn't match. I saw how my early life was a big mismatch, and how I tried to ignore the pain of my realities not matching, of nothing "they" said making sense. Pot was a natural drug for me. I discovered it when I couldn't ignore the pain anymore. With pot I was able to spend fifteen years in a cocoon, somewhat isolated and insulated from the world. I was actually self-medicating to keep going, because reality hurt too much.

That's part of the insidious nature of pot; it cuts people off. But at the beginning there's so much socializing. The change is so gradual you don't see it coming. That kind of pattern is typical of all drugs, but with pot, there's this level of emotional unavailability. For instance, my second child came to us at the height of my usage, and we have the weakest emotional bond of any of the kids. I couldn't be there when I was smoking. And when I was there, my behavior and emotions were inconsistent and unpredictable, similar to what I grew up with in my alcoholic home. I think I knew that on some level, and that helped me finally decide to go for treatment and extra help in therapy.

That first year I was going to aftercare once a week, two meetings a week, seeing my therapist, and seeing my counselor at the treatment center when things got really difficult. My husband was going to Al-Anon, aftercare, and group therapy. He saw changes happening in me fast, and he was afraid I'd grow past him. We made a conscious decision to work on ourselves for two years before we worked on our relationship. We decided our relationship would have a better chance if we each got ourselves to a better place and then tried to work on big issues together, like intimacy. Pot and small kids had made any kind of intimacy a moot issue for a long time.

Another big issue in early recovery was my parenting. My anger was getting to the point where I was being verbally abusive, and I was scared I'd get physically abusive, so we worked a lot on that, especially during PMS times.

I guess another big issue early on was my infertility. I remember feeling like I had a huge hole in my abdomen. It was "empty" in there; it affected how I thought of myself as a woman. I had a lot of mourning to do about that. And on top of all that, we had our house remodeled that first year and adopted our third child. I needed help staying sober through all that.

As time went on, I also worked on the following issues: codependence; being afraid of authority figures; always feeling like "it" (whatever "it" was) was my fault; learning about boundaries—parenting, setting up boundaries with my kids, setting limits in my life; self-esteem issues; arrogance; grief over my mother dying; needing to be the best; being perfect to cover up feelings. We worked on all that stuff.

It took a lot of time and guidance, gentle and not-so-gentle, to get me out of figuring things out in my head and not connecting with my gut. It was like the connection had been severed, and it took incredible efforts to build the road between my head, my heart, and my guts. It was very scary, but I got beneath the layers of defenses I had created and made friends with myself.

I can see why it took five years of individual and group therapy with one therapist and a few years of couple's work. Jonathan and I were in a couple's group that met every other week for about two years, and then saw the male therapist for a year. Jonathan still sees him.

You know my early fear about never being able to make up the twenty years I blew being high? Well, I found out it doesn't exactly work like that. I had to pick up where I had left off, but I really couldn't relive the entire twenty years. As soon as my body and mind were chemically free, reality cropped up. With good guidance, that reality capsule could come up and get worked on. Reality has an internal pressure of its own. In sobriety it's like a pressure cooker; it comes out quicker than when I was stoned. It has its own time sequence that says, "This is the time to do it."

I had alcohol cravings for several months in early recovery. I never had any conscious cravings for pot, although I knew I couldn't be near it (I'd either grab it or run away), but for seven years now, I've had dreams about pot almost weekly. It's the same dream. I find out I never really stopped, that I've been smoking a little all along. I feel really angry that I still have that dream. I think it shows how powerful a drug marijuana is, for me to still have cravings in my dreams seven years later. I don't dream about drinking, and I was definitely an alcoholic.

I still go to meetings. When I hear about people who have eight or twelve years of sobriety and they go back out, I know I need to keep going to meetings. I don't know what would happen if I went home and my brother fired up a joint. Could I let it go by me?

My oldest child is now twelve, entering his teenage years. He's developed into a delightful kid. Actually, all three have. They wouldn't be who they are today if Jonathan and I hadn't gotten into recovery. They've now had recovering parents for seven years—far more than they had us actively practicing our diseases.

The biggest lesson I've learned from A.A. is, it's okay to ask for help. I learned that early on in A.A., and I keep learning and relearning it. There are lots of resources I can use when I need them. Sometimes I have to push myself in a mechanical sort of way. There are always issues to work on; even now, seven years later I can still dig myself into a hole of isolation, and have to dig myself out. But today, with the help of the program, I can do that.

I'm still struggling with connecting, trusting, and intimacy. I see a lot of that as a legacy of pot addiction and growing up as an adult child of an alcoholic (ACA). In the first few years, I was more apt to blame it on being an adult child, but later, the more time I was clean and sober, the more I came to believe that a lot of it was caused by pot's fallout.

Some gifts I've gotten in sobriety are health, sleeping really well at night, and dreaming. Now my dream life is one of the most valuable tools I have for learning about my life. I now have feelings, and can allow them to really be there and be accessible so that I can share them with someone else. I have regained the soft, sensitive person I was before I started smoking pot. That's a really nice part of me. Now I can be with people and not have this secret that I'm with them, but not really, because I'm stoned. I'm really present with others. I'm touched by people, and I can really respond to them. It's a process.

Another thing that's changed since recovery: Now I'm really good in my work, and it's much easier to do. I have a strong, intuitive quality that I can tap into. When I was smoking, I was foggy, but now I'm clear-headed and I enjoy being decisive and intuitive. I can sit down to this huge mishmash of tapes, and somehow it becomes a coherent program of the length it was supposed to be.

There's another aspect of recovery which has to do with spirituality. Intuition is really about Higher Power and not needing to run the show, a pathway that taps into a stronger, more silent and intuitive voice, which isn't necessarily me. It was very noisy in my head in early recovery. I'd look at every possible choice—up and down, in and out; words, words, words, and thoughts, thoughts, thoughts. It took me four years of sobriety to shut off some of the voices in my head. At first the quiet scared me, but then I started to realize that quietness is serenity, and I actually hear a lot more. Choices are a lot more clear now. They just come. That's the most wonderful gift in recovery, not having to figure it all out. There just isn't a lot of verbosity involved. It's definitely based on quietness. A big difference I often see is how I can sit back and listen in the silence. I think a lot of talk in meetings about humility—it was so different than how I was brought up—helped me come back from that unrealistic place where I was supposed to be so special, and ended up so alone in how I dealt with everything. I'm not alone anymore.

The most difficult area is the marriage. That's where the most powerful images and models are. But even in that, we've seen a lot of wonderful changes, and I've gotten a lot of wonderful feelings. It took around three or four years to see significant changes. The kids are such a distraction that it's easy to be the "perfect" parents and ignore each other. Our marriage has room for improvement, but it's a lot better than it was.

When I was stoned, I was basically not receptive to anything that wasn't internal. Sobriety is about receptivity. I had fake boundaries before, in order to feel safe. I was constantly feeling unsafe in early sobriety because there weren't those fake boundaries anymore. Another gift was learning that what makes me feel uncomfortable is what I need to deal with. Today I know I'll be stuck with my uncomfortable feelings until I deal with them. But at least I have them and can deal with them.

I have this sense that I'll be taken care of. I think it has to do with trust, too—trust in myself (and my choices), in other people, and in spirituality. I don't have to second guess so much. I also trust I can handle what happens. That kind of stuff grows slowly, happening over time, yet it seems to somehow grow exponentially as well.

I guess that's a lot for seven years of sobriety. I certainly couldn't have been experiencing this stuff if pot was still in my life.

CHAPTER NINE
Phil

Age 42
Corporate Executive
Eight Years of Sobriety

I was born in the rural South. My mother was eighteen and my father nineteen when I was born. I was their second child. My parents worked really hard. My mother worked in a factory and my father juggled five jobs at once. He'd start working at 5 A.M. and finish at 2 A.M. Despite all that hard work, we were still low-income, rural farmer types. My parents just couldn't get ahead. When I was five, my father ran off and joined the army. I don't blame him. It was the only way he could see to support us.

The thing I remember most about my childhood was being left alone most of the time. We had a baby-sitter who would kick us out of the house about fifteen minutes after my mother left for work, whether it was raining or sunny. She'd let us back in right before my mom came home at night. She neglected to feed us properly. Whatever she was cooking for 5 o'clock dinner, she'd serve us at noon, regardless of its level of preparation —half cooked beans—anything that was convenient for her. My brother and I pretty much grew up on our own, and did not like authority.

My mother tried, but I always considered her "interest" intrusive. Here was someone who was never around, but when she wanted us to, we were supposed to open up and be close. No way. The main philosophy of our family and our extended family was this old-fashioned belief that children should be seen and not heard. When we didn't adhere to that, we'd get spanked. It was a very dry, very unemotional, very detached kind of family, like those you see in old movies. So I never did understand my mother's periodic attempts to get close to us.

I grew up being very sensitive in an environment that didn't appreciate that at all. I liked doing things with people, but that was frowned upon as being weak by my family. If I wanted to do things with friends, then I wasn't being independent enough, according to my family.

After my father was in the army, we moved whenever we could be near him. If there wasn't enough money or he was overseas (in Korea or Vietnam), we went back "home," which meant the rural South. No matter where we were living, my brother and I spent every summer with our grandparents, alternating summers with each set. My father's family was pretty well off. My mother's parents were poor tenant farmers. Moving was hard on me.

My father's grandfather had acquired most of the land in the county during prohibition. Land was a dollar an acre and moonshine was a dollar a bottle. My grandmother was reasonably well off, but among all the kids and grandkids, we never saw any of it, except when we went there for summers. Then we'd have people to boss around, because we were "the master's kids."

I liked the comfort of having well-to-do grandparents, but they were extremely unemotional. I can remember once, when my grandfather was going into town, and my brother and I both wanted to go. He only had room for one of us. He said, "Why don't you two go into the other room and fight it out?" I ended up beating up my brother, which was really something, because I was much smaller than he was. When I came back, my grandfather laughed and took me. That laugh was the only emotion I ever saw him show.

My mother's side of the family was friendlier, but that's also the side of the family in which I started being molested by an uncle when I was five. It went on till I was eight or so. I've had to work that through as an adult. At the time, I thought some attention was better than no attention, so I didn't really feel too bad. On Saturdays, this same uncle would walk two and a half miles to the grocery store with a quarter and come back with twenty-five pieces of penny candy. We'd sit there, thrilled, and divide the candy among ourselves. It was a real treat.

I remember times when we had no money for food. We'd get milk from the cow, and we made cornbread. On Friday nights, we'd cut up tomatoes and onions and put that in the cornbread. Everyone felt like it was a real feast.

I was pretty intelligent, so I always excelled at school. I was a real clean-cut kid, but with all our moving around, I never felt like I fit in. When I was up North, I didn't fit in because I was a Southerner. When I'd go down South again, they'd say I talked like a Yankee. I always thought of myself as an outsider. I never felt connected to a group of people. I believe that has a lot to do with my getting into drugs.

When I was seventeen, we were living in a trailer camp in the South. My father had gone overseas, and we were supposed to meet him in a few months. A friend of my brother's was living with us. One day, he asked me if I wanted to smoke marijuana. I knew nothing about drugs, but I said, "Sure, why not?" I didn't even smoke cigarettes, so the smoking part was hard for me. I don't know if it was really marijuana or oregano. We smoked it all summer, and I never noticed anything, except I didn't like the taste.

One day, he asked me if I wanted to do acid. I thought acid was marijuana in pill form, so I said, "Sure!" I took it on my way to school. When I saw colors going across the classroom, I would say, "Wow, look at the colors!" I dove out my English class window and threw honeysuckle vines in; then sat on my desk making honeysuckle headbands for everyone. Because I was such a clean-cut kid and such a good student, and because everyone was preoccupied by a major school event happening in the afternoon, no one seemed to notice. I managed to go to work and started talking to two girls. I figured, "Drugs! This stuff's great. You have fun. You meet girls. Wonderful stuff!" I feel like I had put all my previous beliefs and values about people and the world to rest that day. I spent the next few years trying to form a new reality about the world.

I had a wonderful summer dating the two girls I had met while I was tripping. Everything was out in the open. It was the most joyous summer of wild abandon and sex. I kept smoking the so-called marijuana, but it didn't do anything to me. I didn't like alcohol so I didn't drink, and I didn't trip again that summer.

We moved overseas at the end of that summer. On my very first day there my father introduced me to a boy he thought would be a good influence on me. The boy invited me out with his friends, and we went somewhere in the woods and smoked hash. Hash was very cheap at twenty-five cents a gram. The first day of school, I met a guy who asked me if I wanted to smoke a joint. I said, "Sure!" It turned out he was the most "in" guy with the drug clique at school. We were friends for the next few years. I was a real part of his clique. For me to be included in a circle of friends was something I had never experienced before. It felt wonderful!

We did drugs just about every night. I figure, in addition to smoking hash all the time, I probably did acid over three hundred times in the next few years. I remember a six-month period when I hadn't gone a day without acid. I finally stopped one day when I was walking around our housing complex and couldn't remember if I had taken acid that day. I decided I wanted to chill out for awhile. I still smoked hash, which was readily available. Marijuana was hard to find and more expensive. We could buy speed in drug stores, so we did that sometimes, but not too much, because we knew a guy who had gotten really fried on the stuff.

After high school I got a job. At the end of the year I decided to join the army. In those days when you joined, you could go where you wanted. I had seen enough guys coming back from Vietnam looking weird that I knew I didn't want to go there. My draft number was so low that I figured I could easily wind up in Vietnam if I didn't join first. I got myself stationed close to Canada, so I could get over the border and escape if they tried to send me to Vietnam.

During the day, I was a clean-cut guy in the army with polished boots, the whole nine yards. Then in the evening, I'd fire up a joint on the way home and spend the evening stoned. I was nineteen.

I ended up getting married to this girl, even though we fought all the time. She was very attractive. I was in the army; I had an army haircut; I looked stupid. I thought, "Do I marry this woman, or do I remain celibate for the next three years?" I remember standing at our wedding, wondering, "How long will this last?" She didn't do drugs. I smoked a lot of grass. In truth, it didn't last very long.

I had grown up believing your word is your bond, and I had said, "Till death do us part." Since I knew I needed to get out of the marriage, I saw death as my only option, and I began to feel suicidal.

I decided to see a marriage counselor; that was 1975. He kept wanting to talk to me about my marijuana use; I wanted to talk about other things. He put me in a group of alcoholics, which I thought was a total waste of time. After a couple of months I walked out. It gave me a really negative attitude towards any sort of therapy.

When I got out of the army, I got a job working for a corporation. My wife and I got divorced. I started working hard and gradually worked my way up through the company. My life consisted of working eight to twelve hours a day, going home to my apartment, smoking a joint, and crashing. On weekends I'd cry, because I had absolutely no life outside of work, and I had no idea how to get a life. I had gotten to a place in my career where my peers didn't seem to get high. I was trapped in a nowhere zone. I considered straight people boring.

I started drinking with peers, because they didn't consider drugs "cool." There was a bar downstairs from work. I really couldn't hold my liquor; never could. I'd get plastered on three or four drinks. In a typical week, I'd have these extremely intense days. I would get people fired, demoted, or transferred. I'd go out for drinks with my staff, wind up drunk, and go home with someone. On weekends I would cry.

My relationships were pretty bad. Women lied to me and had affairs. Pretty crazy stuff. I was emotionally abusive to them and vice versa. I finally left that job after deciding that having affairs with people I worked with was a really bad idea.

I got another job and fell in with a different group of people. I experienced the closest thing to my friends in Germany. We'd have drinks at lunch, which sometimes lasted from 11 A.M. till 5 P.M., although I didn't really like liquor. It either didn't affect me or it made me drunk, but alcohol was cheap and socially acceptable. Maybe once a month I had a pleasant time with it. Marijuana was still an important part of my life. I saw myself as being very sophisticated. I kept my joints in a gold cigarette case. I would pop it open as soon as I got into my car in the evenings.

We'd do mushrooms and cocaine in the evenings. I moved from a dingy ground floor studio apartment to a four bedroom flat. After a month, I sat down and realized I'd spent $1,000 on cocaine. It totally shocked me. I tapered back a lot! For the next year or two, I spent no more than $150 to $200 a month on coke. I enjoyed it, but didn't have to have it.

That was pretty much my pattern: I would get burned out at work, go for drinks, get high on the way home and throughout the evening, and then withdraw for the weekend. I usually went away by myself and had a miserable weekend, half sleeping, drinking lots of coffee, smoking pot, chain-smoking cigarettes, and by Monday I would cope with the world again. It was really hard. That continued for a couple of years.

Physically, things were also getting pretty bad for me. When I'd come home from work and smoke a joint, I'd black out. It was getting to the point where I wouldn't smoke a joint till I was ready to go to sleep at night. Whenever I'd think about anything stressful, my muscles would get tense and I'd get the shakes. I still do today. If I've had an intense, interactive day, as I'm starting to relax, I'll have these little convulsions. At the time, I thought it was the cocaine or that

I wasn't coping with life well. Now I know it's the result of smoking marijuana for so long, and I'm probably stuck with it all my life.

People got on my nerves. When I was stressed, I'd find all kinds of things and people to blame. On the way home, if someone was going slow in front of me, I'd bang into their car with my bumper. I'd do that a lot; it could be a carload of people. My life sucked! I hated work—too political and tense. My social life was these weird, druggie kinds of guys. I began realizing I wasn't coping well.

One of my coworkers was an alcoholic. He'd get himself beaten up fairly regularly and not know how it happened. I convinced him he had to see somebody. I said that if he'd do something to improve his life, I'd do something to improve mine. I was referring to my stress. I thought of it like that, "If I just knew how to deal with stress, I'd be okay." That's why I was smoking grass—because I didn't know how else to unwind.

My friend went off to a thirty-day treatment program and I visited him. When he got out, I offered to see someone about my stress, so he wouldn't feel he was the only person seeing a therapist. My promise to do something for myself gave me the push I needed to seek help, when I couldn't bring myself to do it just for me. I went to the Employee Assistance Program, and said, "Look, I need someone to help me deal with stress." After talking to me for awhile and hearing about my blackouts, she sent me to a therapist [the author], whom I later discovered was a drug counselor.

I remember when we had our first session, and the therapist talked about all these attitudes towards drugs, like, how much fun they were, how much they relieved stress. I understood all of them. I thought the therapist was really cool. I didn't realize until the next week that what she was explaining to me was addiction. I was really disappointed when I finally heard what she was saying in its proper context. I remember arguing with her a lot. I'd say, "I don't have a problem with drugs. Look at all the drugs I've stopped using."

In describing my drug pattern, I would find something I really liked, I would do a little bit, a little bit more, and then use to an extreme excess. Then I'd find I didn't like the effects anymore and switch to something else. Besides, I'd always had insomnia. I'd always smoke something at night to try and relax and fall asleep so I wouldn't have to be up when the birds started singing. Grass was medicinal; not a problem.

When my therapist gave me the book, *Under The Influence*, it was easy for me to find arguments as to how it didn't apply to me. I wasn't an alcoholic, because I really didn't like the alcohol high. I only did it because it was socially acceptable, so I couldn't be an alcoholic, I thought. I remember arguing with my therapist a lot. I didn't think marijuana was addictive. Since I stopped other drugs when they became inconvenient, I figured I could stop smoking pot if I wanted. I was sure I wasn't an addict.

After being in therapy for about a month, I had to attend a corporate meeting out of state. I remember telling my therapist that I wasn't even going to try getting through it without social drinking. During the weekend, someone got credit for a project in which I had played a more significant role. I was really angry. I remember getting into an argument with a woman (who is now my wife). I remember talking to her and not knowing if I was angry because I had a right to be angry, or because I had been drinking. Not knowing where my anger was coming from bothered me a lot! When I came back, I decided to try it my therapist's way. That was nine and a half years ago.

I think I was probably sober a good six to nine months before I really viewed drugs as a problem. They had been part of my life for so long, I didn't know what it was like not to use. I had started when I was seventeen and gone into therapy when I was thirty-two. Being in therapy, being in recovery, and hearing how other people's lives had been dominated by drugs, I started viewing my life differently. Then I started remembering things I had done through the years; things like being furious when I went to my reliable marijuana dealer and he wasn't home. I'd be outraged for the entire evening.

One line in an article my therapist gave me helped convince me that I had a drug problem. It said one of the symptoms of marijuana abuse was a failure to recognize stop signs a person drives by routinely. I kept doing that.

I think my therapist and I really started therapy as opposed to intellectual arguments when we stopped arguing about whether I was an addict. I stayed "dry" and continued going to meetings. We started acknowledging I had other issues than just drugs. I started taking meetings and being in recovery seriously. I was thinking, "It's gotta be better than this;" and my therapist kept saying it was. Even though we weren't talking about drugs *per se*, I started recognizing patterns in my life that matched those of people who considered themselves alcoholics and addicts. After I heard enough of those examples, I got to where I felt I wasn't lying if I'd say I was an addict.

I tried a lot of different meetings. In N.A., they'd talk about "the Joneses," an expression to describe physical withdrawal symptoms such as shaking and sweating: I hadn't had those. In A.A., people talked about all this alcoholic stuff, and I couldn't relate. But when I went to Cocaine Anonymous meetings people talked about themselves as garbage junkies. They'd do anything. It didn't really matter what they did, as long as they had something to get them high. I could relate.

I can remember in early recovery wondering, "How can anyone live a life without drugs? Life sucks. Without drugs, how is one going to deal with all the personal problems? If my therapist could help me fix my personal problems, then I could try to live without drugs." But even as I was thinking that, I was not doing any, because my therapist was still making it a condition of seeing her. I finally got to where I felt like I could begin to look at living life without drugs. That was so hard.

Through the lens of early recovery, I could see the quality of relationships I had had before getting into recovery. I also saw that people in meetings were not religious fanatics. They didn't get high, yet they had fun lives. It was a novel concept. At that point, getting through a day without using was a relief. There was no clear sense of how any of this was going to turn out, but I was just hoping, trying to get through another day.

I don't remember much of my early recovery, only moments—being elected the chairperson of a meeting my first summer, telling my story for the first time. In many ways, my being an outsider stayed with me. I never got a sponsor. I never felt it would be of value to me.

In the beginning, I'd often have to leave meetings during the break. I couldn't stand social interactions. Finally, I felt like I could hang out during breaks. I started socializing with people from the program. I found if I'd go out for coffee with a group after a meeting and end up interested in a woman, at the next meeting I'd be preoccupied wondering about her or wondering what she was thinking. I didn't like how that affected me. I decided I'd take people's advice in meetings and not get involved with anyone during my first year of sobriety. Instead, I started going bowling with groups of people from C.A. meetings.

At the same time, I was working on my stuff in therapy, twice a week, individually and in group sessions. I remember swearing at my therapist about two-thirds of the time in group sessions, because she said something I didn't agree with.

On my thirty-third birthday I had sixty-six days of sobriety. I took my therapist's advice and broke off all my old friendships. I went to C.A. meetings six days a week; sometimes A.A. meetings. I tried one Marijuana Anonymous meeting. I could see myself in the people at M.A.—the lethargy, indifference, slowness—but I couldn't stand being around it. Most of them were like the TV commercial, where they were still living at home saying, "Geez, nothing ever changes." At the time, I was a vice president in a large corporation and just couldn't relate to how stuck they were. It was too bad, because I felt like otherwise our stories matched.

I had initially decided to avoid relationships during my first year of sobriety, but I did start dating a woman I was working with when I was clean for about six months. We were working on a number of different projects and traveling around the country together. We ended up getting married and now we have a son who's almost three years old. But back to then...

When I had about nine months of sobriety, I threw away all my paraphernalia and my last bag of marijuana. It had taken me that long to acknowledge that this wasn't a temporary lifestyle change. Around that time I started saying, "Okay, I'm an addict. I'll work on that."

I continued therapy. In fact, I'm still in therapy. When we moved, I had to find a new therapist. I was very active in C.A. for awhile, but the politics annoyed me. In therapy I'm still working on the issues that make it so hard for me to socialize and make friends.

Right now, I'm working at my job too much. I come home drained. I don't have a lot of energy left for my wife and son. I'm feeling tired tonight, so I'm having trouble coming up with some of the joys of sobriety. I know I went through a period where I recognized the richness of sobriety, but I'm not in touch with them right now.

How is life different now from when I was using? It's so different that it's difficult to compare. I remember how freeing it was the first time I saw a police car, and I thought, "So what?" I can remember in recovery when I broke through a certain dollar threshold in my checking account, which I'd never been able to get through before. While I was using, I made very good money, but it all went to living high on the hog, like flying to a different city for dinner on the spur of the moment and other things like that. I guess within two years or so, I'd saved up enough money with my wife that we were able to buy a house. We had both entered the relationship with nothing. Now we have money set aside for our son's college education.

I'm still uncomfortable around people who drink heavily and somewhat uncomfortable around people who are drinking at all. I assume they're going to drink heavily. I tend to shy away from situations where people will be drinking.

Having a Higher Power has always been a struggle for me. Growing up with a religiously fanatic mother and a religiously indifferent but puritanical father didn't help. Despite my troubles with the concept, I've definitely used my Higher Power from time to time.

One of the hardest parts of recovery was getting through the Twelve Steps. I finally got to where I could view a Higher Power as more of an internal part of myself that I can't talk to directly. There are times when I let things go and see how they work out. I'm assuming I'm turning it over to that part of me where I choose to see my Higher Power residing. That's as close as I've come to accepting a Higher Power. I'm feeling less spiritual this month than I have at other times.

Before I got into recovery, I was actually tired of my old lifestyle. I just didn't know how else to live. So the differences are really big. I just wish I felt more of the joy I have felt at different times. Work has been so stressful and busy for the last six months. I guess I've let it kind of swallow me up. When I was going to meetings, I could balance better, but even then I was battling the tendency for work to overtake me. I'd like that to be different.

I'm in this coasting mode. I'm not having any highs or lows. I need to live differently because I'm not really enjoying life as much as I have in other years of my sobriety. I'm not going to meetings right now. I kept trying meetings for about a year and a half after I moved here, but I couldn't find a meeting I felt connected to. I was far enough along in sobriety that I just wasn't getting the joy from listening to all the newcomers. Perhaps I should go back. My wife always encouraged me to go, because even when I went to a meeting I didn't like, I would come home mellower than when I left. So it might be something I need to do.

There have been good changes, like with my son. He truly doesn't buy any excuses. What my day is like really doesn't matter (to him). He's taught me to be cognizant of what's going on with someone else. I have a tendency to expect everyone to adjust to me, and John doesn't.

When I'm with him, it brings up my sensitivity in a good way. I can tell when I'm in tune with him. For example, if we're going shopping and John wants to pick up something to eat, I know my five-minute shopping trip has just turned into a twenty-minute shopping trip. I can let that be, because I want him to be happy and feel accepted and grow. To be able to give that to him, not because he expects that of me, but because I want to, is something I've enjoyed. In the past if I gave that to someone in a relationship, it would be because I wanted them to think of me in a certain way. There would have been some ulterior motive. I don't want to deprive him of feeling accepted, because I feel like I had so little of that.

He's taught me that adults are like children. When John gets upset, it may or may not have anything to do with me, especially at his age. I can know it's nothing personal and I can help him, or I can get upset with him, which accomplishes nothing. Before, I always assumed that when people around me were upset, it was because of me. I'd react in a defensive, angry, or insecure manner.

Being sober and watching my son has made me more tolerant of other adults. I've learned to shift my reference point from my perspective being the only valid one, to looking at someone else's point of view and working with it, instead of coldly imposing mine. I can also help bridge the gap when other people are not seeing eye-to-eye. When I was using, I'd go from being a fun-loving drinking buddy to firing someone in a heartbeat for some small transgression. I certainly couldn't relate to another person and understand his or her perspective.

I've heard about people in recovery reparenting their inner child. With John, I feel like he lets me be good to him and, as a result, I'm being better for me. I find I'm giving myself more permission to be me because I give him permission to be himself. Now I can give myself permission to be introverted and take the time I need for myself, instead of thinking, "Oh, God, I have to overcome this!" It's been wonderful. I feel so fortunate that he has a lot of me in him, and I can look at him and make it be okay. It's because I know he deserves the acceptance and, as a result, I know I deserve acceptance, too.

I've learned to accept my need for boundaries. When I need space I ask for it. My wife understands that Friday nights are for videos and quiet nights at home. My boss and coworkers understand that if we are having a people-intensive conference, I will not join people for lunch. I'll point them in the right direction for restaurants, but then I'll go back to my room to recharge. I'm no longer angry at myself for being a social wimp.

I feel so fortunate that I was an addict, because I got to go to therapy and be in recovery, instead of just living my life as a cold workaholic, which is my family's pattern. If I had kept on the track I was on, there would have come a day when I'd look at my child and say, "Want to go camping, what's-your-name?" I feel so fortunate that I get to actually watch my son grow up. It's good that I'm cherishing this, because I know I could have stayed numb and angry and missed it altogether.

The level of comfort I have with myself is so amazing, given how I felt for so long. I know this isn't the best time in my life, but it sure beats the angry, rigid addict who tried hard to have fun and still felt lousy, alone, and angry. So I think I'll try going to meetings again; they did help. Maybe I can get back to that happy, joyous, and free state I've been in earlier in recovery. It's worth the effort.

CHAPTER TEN

Margie

Age 43
Small Business Owner
Twelve Years of Sobriety

I grew up in a suburban section of a large city. We all had our 40 X 100 foot plots. It was a pretty safe area, but we were never allowed out after dark. Even when it was dark around 4:30 P.M. in the winter, we were cautioned about the "dangers" of living in a big city. Our family was a regular old family. My dad worked and my mom stayed home. I had two siblings. We sometimes got along great and sometimes fought a lot. I think one thing I knew for sure when I was growing up was that I was loved. Our parents sometimes had very emotionally charged ways of showing love, but we never doubted that they loved us. That part of growing up always felt good to me.

I think that because of some of the emotional ups and downs at our house, I had a sense of unpredictability in my life. That, in combination with always listening to the news at dinner (which seemed to be about burglaries, homicides, rapes, and suicides in a big city) filled me with fears. I was a pretty scared kid. I certainly had more fears than my siblings. But other than being scared a lot, I was very happy, outgoing, and full of questions.

I have a lot of early memories from when I was growing up. They center around the house and our family, playing with my brothers, my cousins, friends. Our house was always open. People popped in and out. There was always plenty of home-cooked food to share. I remember dinner parties where my mother was hostess and my father bartender. He never did a very good job. My mother always had to remind him to offer people a second drink. He'd say, "Why would they want a second drink?" and my mother would say, "Some people just do." So he'd offer and usually have a few takers. My parents often split a beer with dinner. That was the extent of their drinking.

I remember first hearing about marijuana in junior high school. It was under the guise of, "If you're ever offered weird, hand-rolled cigarettes, don't smoke them; they might have drugs in them and make you crazy!" That was easy to stay away from. But when I started hearing more and more about it in high school from people who had actually smoked it, pot didn't sound so drastic at all. In fact, of all the drugs going around—acid, mescaline, uppers, downers, speed—pot seemed the most benign.

Somehow, I went from this innocent kid who had a really good, solid head on her shoulders to someone who wanted to do something everyone was doing. But I sure didn't want to get in trouble. I kept hearing pot was harmless, that it wasn't a drug; it was natural, more like an herb, kind of like a spice. I began to think of it as the only thing I could do and stay safe with. When I turned fifteen, I tried to figure out how I could get hold of some. I also wanted to try it for the first time in the "right" circumstances, which to me felt like with someone I trusted and someplace where my parents wouldn't find out. I was a little scared of trying it, but mostly I was very intrigued.

Maybe I should say a little more about myself before I started smoking pot. I showed good judgment, clear thinking. I was considered precocious by many adults, but I don't think my father started trying to get me to see the world in moderation or to make compromises until after I was smoking pot. I think I was a pretty solid thinker before. I had a critical mind; I could reason; I could see both sides of a story.

I lost those abilities when marijuana came into my life, but I sure didn't know that when I was using. In fact, I would have argued with you till I was blue in the face that I was a better thinker, more open to new ideas, when I was high than when I had been straight all those years—all those years till I was fifteen-and-a-half.

I finally found someone I could trust to get me some marijuana and do it with me the first time. I was still a little afraid, but I also couldn't wait. It took me five joints till I felt anything, but then that "buzz" took over, and we talked and talked in a way that was new for me. We also made out behind my garage, which was not something I was accustomed to doing. Before that first time of smoking pot, when I'd go out with a boy, I'd spend half the date trying to figure out how I could get back home, get me in the house, and him out of the house without having to kiss him goodnight. So to be making out was very new for me. I liked it—that extra chemistry going. Being sexually active behind pot was a theme that persisted throughout my pot-smoking years.

It's funny, looking back, because when I first started smoking pot, I thought everyone was smoking pot. I knew it was all around me. Yet I was one of the first in my circle of friends to do it. My thinking was already distorted, wanting to do it because "everyone" was, and so it must be okay.

Unfortunately, my thinking didn't fit reality, but I didn't know that at the time.

I smoked whenever I could in high school, which wasn't that often. I baby-sat regularly but had other hobbies to spend my money on. Maybe once every other week or so, I'd smoke if it was offered, but I didn't go out of my way to have it.

I worked hard in college, with part-time jobs and full-time school; living at home, trying to be a "good girl," but lying about a lot of my behavior because I knew my parents would be upset, scared, and angry. I didn't like lying, but I had to survive at home. I avoided my parents as much as possible. They came to resent the way I was using the house as a "hotel" rather than being a real member of a family. And I, in turn, resented their attempts to re-engage me in family life, which I considered to be unnecessary intrusions in my life. The more they asked of me, the more I lied. The more I lied, the more I didn't like myself, especially the fact that it was getting easier for me to lie. The more I didn't like myself, the more I smoked pot to escape those feelings.

During my third semester of college, I went out with a guy who had very easy access to pot. He introduced me to the concept of a "wake-up joint." I liked it. That semester, I smoked all through the day, from early morning till my last joint to help me sleep. I did very well in school, but I don't even remember what courses I took. I know I worked and went to school, but the whole semester is a blur in my mind.

At the end of the semester, he left town, but not before leaving me with a few ounces of pot, which I assumed would last me the whole summer. Two weeks later, the bag was empty, and I plunged into a major depression. I missed the pot when I ran out. I didn't like missing the pot. I remember struggling to get up in the morning and go to work. I was bummed the whole summer. At first, I thought maybe I was depressed because my boyfriend had moved away, but I had to admit I didn't really miss him, just the pot. Life was really okay; I liked my job, but I couldn't stop being depressed. I did get clear-headed enough to realize my depression was probably from smoking so much pot (since I had never felt like that before). I decided that pot wasn't good for me and that I wasn't going to smoke it anymore. I was eighteen. I had been smoking pot for two and a half years. I felt good about my decision.

At the end of the summer, I transferred to a college far from home and started working more hours to pay for the difference in tuition. When I started my new school, I found friends who didn't smoke, or who smoked occasionally and didn't pressure me to use. I worked hard at my studies and my work to support myself in school. My strained relationship with my parents eased. They were pleased that I had become so responsible and was making it so far from home. I was pleased with myself, too, even though my schedule was so hectic that if I had one weekend afternoon off where I wasn't studying or working, I considered myself lucky. I found juggling all of that a lot easier without smoking pot, because I had my whole mind to work with.

A few years later, in graduate school, I got in with this crowd where one person grew pot and was giving it to his friends. I think I was getting tired of working so hard and was having trouble falling asleep. Someone said smoking pot made it easier to fall asleep. I remembered that. I said I'd like to try it, and a friend gave me an ounce. I tried it and, sure enough, it did the trick, but I was careful to use it only medicinally before bedtime. I did that for a long time, every night.

Gradually, I started breaking my rule of only smoking pot every night just before going to sleep. I always had a good justification for doing it some other time, but the exceptions started happening more frequently. Weekends were okay, parties were okay, new dates became okay, stressful afternoons became okay. In my head, my pot smoking was still medicinal. By then, I had forgotten that, at eighteen, I had known that pot wasn't good for me. In fact, I didn't remember that until my mid-thirties and I had been clean and sober for about four years.

Drinking was something I didn't like at first. In college I had to force myself to drink a beer, because I really didn't like the taste. It wasn't until graduate school, at conferences and other gatherings, that older friends introduced me to mixed drinks, and I began to enjoy alcohol. By my late twenties, I had a great bar at home (in a kitchen cabinet) and had two kinds of pot in my freezer. I'd panic if I'd get "seriously low," and buy more. I never ran out!

Professionally, I was a young hotshot in my field; I was successful. On the personal side, I always had at least one boyfriend. They'd last anywhere from two weeks to two years, one right after the other, sometimes overlapping. Pot was something I used, but only "after all my responsibilities were met." Somehow, I went along like this. Gradually, what was different was, I forgot how it felt to be a carefree teenager, that kid who liked herself, that kid who woke up in the morning with a clear head and conscience, that kid who was open to a lot of different types of people and ideas. I was in a rut and didn't know it. I didn't like myself. I knew that every morning and I knew it every night. In between, I filled my days with activity and filled my nights with people, so I didn't have to feel what I felt inside. It still crept in and surprised me every once in awhile, so I'd smoke some more pot and complain to a friend. I remember, especially around my birthday, hoping I'd be happier the next year, but from the outside I was doing fine. I was successful. I had a nice apartment. I lived in a beautiful place. I had a boyfriend (usually). I looked good.

I remember when I started not enjoying pot so much. It was soon after being introduced to cocaine. That stuff made me too hyper. One day, when I was thinking I'd go get some coke around the corner because I was tired, it hit me. Here I was, going to get some coke when, usually, if I was tired, I'd get a cup of coffee. I knew I was in trouble with cocaine, so I stopped. It was around that time I started talking to friends about how much more I was drinking (every day) than I used to drink (occasionally), and how smoking pot wasn't quite "cutting it" anymore. When I told them I was worried about how my use had escalated, they told me not to worry because, after all, I used less than most of them. That was true, but it also said a lot about the people I had surrounded myself with. Yes, they used more than I did, but what they didn't know was that my body has always metabolized drugs differently than most people. In addition, just because I used less than they did, that didn't mean I didn't have a problem. Their solution for the fact that pot wasn't cutting it anymore was to turn me on to new sources for better pot. Solution? No. Enabling? Yes. But at that time, I didn't know what that word meant.

Every once in awhile, when I was home alone smoking pot, I'd feel paranoid; like, I'd think I heard suspicious noises and have to go check them out and be really scared as I checked them out. I also had trouble falling asleep when I was stoned because of all the scary and lousy thoughts I'd get as I tried to unwind. Pot didn't help; in fact, it made it worse. But I kept smoking it anyway. I was used to it helping and I wanted it to work again; I really did.

That went on for two years. By the end, I had cut back from every day to every three or four days, and all that was happening was that I was feeling paranoid less often but unhappy most of the time. I wanted to stop, but couldn't get myself to be "seriously low" and not buy more.

Then this crazy thing happened. I met a guy who didn't do any drugs. He didn't even drink; he hadn't in a long time. I was sure I'd be bored with him and this would be a two-week relationship. For years I had certainly rejected any other guys who didn't use, knowing they'd be boring. But this one was different. He seemed to know how to have fun. I had fun with him. I giggled; I laughed. I didn't feel bad; I didn't hurt inside. I didn't feel like I was on an emotional roller coaster.

I didn't smoke for a few days. I didn't smoke for a week; I didn't smoke for a few weeks. I decided to try a month without any pot and without any drinking. I liked it. I liked waking up in the morning without a horrible taste in my mouth. My body didn't feel like it was stuffed with cotton anymore. I could feel my muscles moving. I felt more clear in my mind.

It was a month of not using. It was two months; it was three. It was a year; it was a year and a half. I started going to A.A., realizing I had crossed over the line from abuse into addiction without having known it. The only way I realized that was by having more and more memories come back after I stopped using, and all the memories defied my rules of who I wanted to be and how I behaved. Once I wasn't "self-medicating" anymore, I couldn't fight reality, and my memories of how I had been living for the last ten years began flooding in.

I finally came to realize I had been a successful alcoholic and addict who had succeeded in fooling herself about what she was doing. The denial I experienced was no different than any other alcoholic or addict experiences. It was insidious, detailed, and justified, but I was lying to myself by distorting the truth to fit my pot-induced reality. I suppose I could have felt very ashamed of some of my behavior through the years, but I learned enough about this disease to know it wasn't me per se. It was a drug-induced me operating from a distorted reality. I was able to forgive myself early on for some pretty dumb choices I had made. I didn't hold any grudges. It just fueled my desire to be drug free so I could make the kinds of decisions I would be proud of.

I didn't take easily to the program; I didn't like it. I couldn't say the word *God.* I didn't believe in God. I couldn't even say *Higher Power.* What I did know was, going to the countryside always helped me feel less stressed, so I used Mother Nature as my Higher Power till I could say the word God. It took me a good three years or so till I stopped stumbling over that word.

Now, I love how much less angry I am as a human being and how much easier life is when it's not all on my shoulders and I can ask for help, ask for lessons when things don't go my way, and accept life on its own terms rather than fighting life to fit into my terms. I always used to have to learn the hard way, banging my head against a brick wall till I finally realized something. Now, I can usually see the brick wall and make choices about how I want to deal with it. I'm still ambitious, but in a less frantic way. I'm still successful, but I put the emphasis on balance and family rather than personal achievement. I'm not always successful in the balance department, but it is a high priority.

When I first started to flirt with the idea that maybe I should give up drinking alcohol and smoking pot in my early thirties, I couldn't imagine what life would be like without them. I had forgotten that, from eighteen till about twenty-one, I had had a few good years not smoking pot. In my mid-twenties, there was another year when I again didn't like the effects I was experiencing from pot and stopped using. But by my thirties, I was so scared that life would be boring without marijuana. I had forgotten I could and had lived without it. I couldn't imagine going one week without using; a few days might be okay, but not one week.

Recently I had my twelfth A.A. birthday. Now, if that isn't a miracle, I don't know what is.

Has life been boring? Anything but boring. I've learned so much, so much in all areas. Personally, I'm much more easy going and less driven. I have a great sense of humor again. I read. I participate in sports. I go to movies. I go to plays. I have friends. And I remember the events I've been to. I have a longstanding partnership with a very nice man. I'm a mother and I love that more than anything in this world. I can see what's in front of my face, and, when I'm confused or I'm in emotional pain, I know "this too shall pass," and I look for signs of what to do. I ask for help, I accept help, and I muddle through without self-medicating. Yes, things that happen in life hurt incredibly sometimes, but it's real, genuine, pure emotional hurt, which won't kill me. It may give me insomnia for awhile, but my soul, my spirit, my being is free. And for that I am very grateful.

Professionally, I've chosen a different path than my formal education prepared me for, but I'm happy with my choices. I enjoy my work. It's fulfilling and not overly taxing. I have energy for my family, which is my first priority.

It's funny, at many points in my earlier life, I would have viewed my life today as "trite," "confining," "much too middle class," "too straight," and probably "boring." I would have been haughtily judgmental. I would have seen my old lifestyle as much more "cool," but it wasn't. I'd much rather be me today, than the me I was trying to be. I could kind of pull that one off, but it sure made me unhappy when I was honest with myself.

I don't feel like I'm struggling to be something I'm not. This feels natural and wonderful to me. For so long, I wondered things like: Could I ever be monogamous? It's been easy. Could I ever have a lasting relationship with a man who treated me well? My relationship hasn't always been easy, but it's definitely been worth the time and effort.

I have not changed the world as I set out to do in the sixties, but I have changed *my* world. I want to live my life with as much honesty and integrity as possible. I like being able to stand behind everything I say and do.

Life's not perfect. I've gone through some very difficult times in recovery. But with my new support system of family, friends, the Twelve Steps of A.A., which provide powerful tools that allow me to do life differently, and a strong relationship with my Higher Power reminding me that whatever I am experiencing will not last forever, I've been able to get through all those bad times without using.

I'm not sure if I really want to tell this part of my story, but I think enough other recovering people have experienced similar things that I guess I should share this part too. Last year, after experiencing the worst year I'd had since getting into recovery, I finally realized something that I think my Higher Power had been trying to tell me for months. I had had some physical problems, which the doctors tried to correct with a strong hormone treatment. The hormones sent me into an emotional tailspin, the likes of which I've never seen! In all fairness, I also had experienced several emotional and physical losses during that time which took their own emotional toll on me. After battling with major depressions that sent me very low four times, as I started going down for the fifth time and found myself involuntarily crying for hours about nothing and not being able to stop, I called for extra help. I didn't want to. I didn't like the idea, but I had to, because I knew I had no emotional reserve left to help me through that one.

I consulted with a psychiatrist who reassured me that from what I was saying (which was all true), it was clear I had marvelous coping skills and incredible tools from being in A.A. so long. But I had a chemical imbalance that I could not will away. She prescribed a very low dose of Prozac. Within a week, I was feeling like myself again. I had wanted A.A. and my life experience to be enough. It was a pride thing, really. But I'm glad I gave in. I was able to become healthier physically and I got my strength back, which the hormone treatment had zapped. I guess one of the things is, when you need drugs, use them as a doctor prescribes. I used to be my own doctor who prescribed marijuana and alcohol when I wanted them, at my own prescribed dose. Now I follow the real MD's orders.

I guess there are a lot more alcoholics and addicts who also have clinical depression than "normal" people, because it's all tied in with the brain chemistry and imbalances in the brain. It sure was hard for me to admit I needed real medicine. I was particularly afraid because I used to look at pot as medicinal.

After a year of medication, I wanted to see what I was like without Prozac. I was hoping my chemistry had readjusted itself. I was able to stop taking the Prozac three months ago and I feel fine.

Besides that one awful, medically-induced imbalance of that year, I've had so many wonderful times: getting married, starting a family, watching my family grow, changing career paths, traveling, meeting new people. And we've been able to do all that without using drugs. Yes, we've had celebrations, only we don't use champagne. We talk, we laugh, we giggle, sometimes we go to special places, sometimes we drink sparkling grape juice mixed with sparkling water. I don't feel deprived. I used to think I'd feel deprived if I couldn't drink a fine wine with dinner, have the latest bud, or sit in front of a fire with a glass of brandy. But it really isn't the bud, the brandy, or the wine that makes a fine evening. It's the people, the ambiance, the feelings, the sharing going on. So, no, I'm not deprived of anything.

Every day that I wake up clean and sober and go to sleep clean and sober, I feel like I've made a choice and have been given a reprieve. I'd much rather choose this drug-free life than go back to how I used to feel on a daily basis, depressed, lonely, alone, like I had to do it all by myself if "it" (whatever "it" was) was going to happen. And when I did it all by myself and it didn't happen, I'd be angry and resentful of whatever I perceived had gotten in my way. I did a lot of blaming and I was angry a good deal of the time. I don't feel like that anymore. I'm not alone. I don't have to do it alone. I have lots of supports to help me through life and with life. I hope to continue having them, using them, enjoying them, appreciating them, and being grateful for their presence.

I like this life; I don't miss the other. I feel a mixture of pride and gratitude that I can be a recovering addict and alcoholic rather than living a roller-coaster life, predicated

147

on high drama, where I survived from one bottom to another. You know, most addicts die using, or from a related accident. At least so far, that doesn't look like it'll have to be my fate. If I keep doing what it takes to stay clean and sober, I will stay clean and sober. And, God willing, my children will see that life can be fun and challenging without drugs, and they will escape the disease which may be waiting silently in their genes.

I'm very grateful that my partner and best friend also happens to be my husband and also shares a drug-free lifestyle. It has made it easier for me, especially at the beginning. It's nice not to have to deal with liquor or drugs in my house at all. I rarely come into contact with it. When I do, I simply say, "No, thank you" or "I don't drink." Last year on July Fourth, I smelled marijuana for the first time in years, and laughed. Who would have ever thought I would be able to go on so long without smelling the essence of marijuana?

I never imagined the life I have. I never thought life could be this good, but it is. My husband and I often turn to each other and say, "Life doesn't get much better than this." Of course, I'm not always that positive; I have my struggles. Balancing is an art I'm better at sometimes and not so great at other times. But at least I'm usually in touch with what is happening, or at least open enough to people around me who say, "Slow down!"

I can't count the number of surprises I've had in recovery. I feel more like I did when I was a little kid than I did between the ages of twenty-two and thirty-two. I am technically "middle aged," but I feel too alive for that. Most days, I like life a lot. Sometimes it feels a bit much, but it's always worth living.

I used to think I had a high "bottom." I didn't lose a job; I didn't lose my home; I wasn't out on the street. I didn't get any DUIs, but I do remember driving home and congratulating myself for not hitting a parked car. I do remember feeling depressed and having no good reason for feeling that way. I did lose my self-respect. And I'm sure if some people were honest with me, I lost their respect along the way, but those people are no longer in my life. They left when I wasn't paying any attention. My bottom was my own. It was low enough that I didn't want to feel that way anymore. It was low enough that, even though I had no idea what life would be like without using, I knew I had to give it a try. So far, these first twelve years have been great. I think I'll stick around and see what else I can learn.

CHAPTER ELEVEN

Jillian

Age 38
Corporate Professional; Small Business Owner
Fifteen Years of Sobriety

I grew up in a large city on the Atlantic Ocean. My mother was a strict Italian Catholic. My mother was very meek around my father, who had an extremely violent temper. He was quite a difficult person to be around. He had been married before and had two grown children. He had been violent with his first family, doing things regularly like banging their heads against a wall. He had thrown one out in his late teens; the other left when he was thirteen. We didn't have a lot to do with his children. I was raised as an only child.

When I was very young, I remember always being afraid of what was going to happen next. My father didn't drink, but you never knew when he was going to erupt and go crazy—totally crazy—throwing things, hitting, screaming; he had no emotional control. My mother was afraid of him, too. There was a lot of tension from not knowing when the violence would hit.

My parents always worked a lot, so I spent a lot of time by myself. When I was less than a year old, they put me in day care. Later, when I was around seven or eight, I was allowed to take care of myself. That meant I had to come straight home from school. I wasn't allowed out again, because there wasn't anyone around to watch me. I became very self-sufficient. I'd play dress-up in my room, being a princess, a queen, or a big star. I tended to stay away from other kids even when I could play with them. It wasn't something I was used to, and I sort of preferred my own company.

At about that time, I started eating a lot. I could eat all afternoon. I didn't like myself or my life. My mother always used to say things like, "The neighbors know; they can all hear your father screaming. I'm so ashamed; everybody knows how bad we are. Everybody knows how low-class we are. They all look down on us because of your father." I grew up feeling ashamed and uncomfortable. Those feelings filled me, and food was my first way of comforting myself.

When I was about ten or eleven, I decided I was tired of being a hefty kid, and I started starving myself. I got to the point where I was maybe eating three hundred calories a day. I'd eat by myself at school, almost coveting my apple lunch. One teacher who really liked me expressed some concern, but there was nothing she could do. This was also the first time I remember being depressed. I spent a lot of time feeling uncomfortable, inadequate, and ashamed. Despite always having the highest grades in school, I still felt really awful.

When I was twelve, I went to spend the night at a girl-friend's house. I ended up drinking an enormous amount. It was my first experience with alcohol. I got violently ill and passed out. I was sick for two days afterwards. My parents were very angry at me. After that episode I started getting really wild at school. I skipped out of Catholic school to hang out with the wild kids from public school. I wore a lot of make-up. I smoked pot for the first time. A girlfriend and

I smoked together, and I remember thinking, "This pretty much doesn't feel like anything." But I kept smoking it whenever I could.

It was the early seventies. I stole sleeping pills from my parents. They relaxed me. I smoked pot when I could. I didn't drink much. By fourteen I was finding a lot of street drugs, Quaaludes, acid. Marijuana was always in the picture. It wasn't even like doing drugs. It was like brushing my teeth; I just did it. I didn't see it as a drug. It was simply an important part of my life, my routine. I loved it.

I think what exacerbated everything was this awful feeling of being uncomfortable, unworthy. Just always feeling less than. And that felt very painful, except when I was high. With pot I didn't care, so I hurt less.

I dropped out of Catholic school and went to public high school. I always had boyfriends. I was very loose morally. Some of that was from drugs, but it was also the times. In the seventies, everyone was doing it. It was the cool thing to fit in. I really wanted to fit in, and the bottom line was, I didn't value myself enough not to do whatever someone wanted.

In high school, I met this really nice guy who was in a college a few hours from my home. I went with him for about four years. He never knew that while he was away in college, I wasn't the good girl he imagined me to be. I went out all the time. I could pull off the nice girl image for short periods of time when he was home. I had manners. I could play the faithful girlfriend. He was really into smoking pot, so I didn't have to hide that part of my life. His college friends were drinking beer, so I started drinking tons of beer. I was having a great old time.

The day I graduated from high school, I left home and moved in with him. I didn't have a job. I'd be stoned from the time I woke up till the time I went to bed. Or drunk. The difference was, I wouldn't drink alone, but I would smoke alone. Everyone was doing the hippie thing, and I was being a hippie. About four or five months later, my boyfriend said maybe I should go to school or get a job. I got a job or two, but they didn't work out. Working interfered with my smoking and my hanging out. I had no sense of anything in life, except partying and having fun. I started feeling resentful that my boyfriend wasn't letting me just get high and do my little hippie thing.

I started thinking that the best thing would be to go back to my parents' house where I could live in this safe place and have my own way, partying freely without this jerk (who was really a nice guy) telling me I had to work or go to school. I decided I'd be happy if I did that. So I left.

When I got back home, I was extremely depressed. I stopped eating. I lost a lot of weight. I stopped drinking, but I didn't stop smoking pot. In fact, that's all I did. My parents were supporting me because I had started college. After about a semester I started getting very paranoid. I remember thinking, "Now I'm going to clean up my act. I'm not going to drink. I'm not going to do drugs anymore." I stopped drinking and doing street drugs, but that didn't mean giving up pot. I honestly didn't see pot as a drug.

I got very interested in school for awhile, maybe two semesters. Then one night a girlfriend asked me to go out and party with her at this private club. I did. Up until then, while I was "cleaning up my act," I was pretty much staying by myself, smoking and studying. The next thing I knew, I had really started partying again, going out all the time, staying up all night. By the next semester, I had dropped out of school, was working at the private club, hanging out, getting crazy, still living at home.

By this time, I had inherited my mother's low self-esteem and my father's bad temper. My mother was afraid of me because, if she would tell me how to behave, I would really let her have it. There was no talking to me! I did what I pleased and had this attitude, "Just try and do anything about it." If they did, we'd have violent fights. I knew my father couldn't kick me out as he had done with his first family, because my mother would protect me. In many ways I had it great there: I had a roof over my head; I had money; I had food; I had a car. I came and went as I pleased. The downside was that sometimes I had to endure violent fights and arguments, but I was used to them.

From the time I was eighteen or nineteen till the time I got sober when I was twenty-three, I was totally high all the time. I had boyfriends. I always picked guys as wild as I was. I was never, ever without pot. I smoked all day, beginning before I went to work, on my lunch hour, after work, and before sleep. I lived stoned. Once in a while I thought about my drinking, and thought, "People who drink like me are alcoholics," but I never questioned the pot.

I remember one morning, after being out all night, talking to a girlfriend about some jerk she had met the night before. We started talking about all these guys we knew who were jerks. I turned to her and in a moment of clarity said, "Did you ever think it might be us? Did you ever think that we have a problem the way we drink and the craziness we get into?" She said, "Nah, nah, it's them." I said, "Yeah, yeah, it's them." There went the moment of clarity.

In my early twenties I became a fanatical runner and a vegetarian. I didn't see any contradiction between my new healthy lifestyle and smoking pot. I'd run in the morning before work and in the evening after work, but before I ran, I always smoked a joint. I was feeling better and moved into an apartment. I mostly saved my real craziness for the weekends.

Somewhere in there, after trying to cut back on drinking several times because it interfered with my running, I sought alcohol counseling on my own. I kept making commitments to my counselor not to drink for three or four weeks. But I never told her about the pot. To me, marijuana wasn't part of the problem. I never intended to stop smoking.

I wasn't very good at keeping my commitments about abstaining from alcohol. I was partying hard again. One day at work I looked down at my desk and realized I couldn't make any sense of the papers. I knew I couldn't function. I was falling apart from all the partying. I picked up my bag and walked out. I had to give up my apartment and move back with my parents. I was very paranoid. I stayed in my room and smoked a lot.

A few months later, I started getting my strength back and was able to get another job. I was trying not to drink, because I knew that was a problem, but I was still doing a lot of sleeping pills and pot. The new job was a really good opportunity. I just knew I would screw it up.

I started drinking more and not being able to work well the next day. I finally started going to A.A. meetings just to keep myself off the streets. I went for a few months and then decided I couldn't handle that anymore. I hated A.A. I hated the whole thing about God. I started drinking again. By this time I had no friends left. I'd go to work. I'd stay focused there because somehow, the paranoia didn't play a part there. But out in the world, I was paranoid.

One day I got extraordinarily drunk. When I got home, a friend I had met in A.A. called to see how I was doing, and I told her I needed help. I started going to A.A. meetings. I got a sponsor. I never drank again, but I was still smoking. After a few weeks, I got the feeling that smoking pot and doing pills weren't acceptable. I didn't talk about it at A.A. meetings, but I did talk to my sponsor. She talked to other people in the program who told her she had to tell me to stop. But, instead, she told me I'd need to give it up when I was ready. I remember calling my sponsor after I was in A.A. for a month and saying, "I just flushed my pot down the toilet." It was a very traumatic thing for me.

To this day, I don't think about drinking or pills much at all. It doesn't bother me to be around alcohol. But pot was, like, my best friend, and I'm still nervous about that. Once in a while, if I'm in a place where someone's smoking pot, it's still, "Oh, my God, help!"

When I got to A.A. and people were talking about life being unmanageable, it hit me that everything I had always wanted my life to be, it wasn't. Everything I had tried to accomplish I had failed at. Life was unmanageable. My whole life was going down the tubes. I didn't want to be known as "Crazy Jillian" anymore. I realized I didn't want to be that person anymore.

I wasn't sure if there was any kind of Higher Power out there when I first started going to A.A. Then I realized that for two weeks I hadn't had a drink. I knew I couldn't have done it on my own. I had tried for years without success. It was miraculous. It made me believe there was something out there helping me.

I've been in the program fifteen years now. Life has changed 180 degrees. There's no comparison, really. I love my life. I took awhile to get here, but it's great.

When I first came to A.A., I really devoted myself to the Steps, to recovery. I made A.A. the most important thing in my life. For years it was the main thing in my life. I had my work, my meetings, and friends from the program. I didn't expand outside of A.A. in terms of friendships. I didn't date a lot. After a long time of immersing myself in A.A., I had to realize I was afraid of being crazy again, so I was isolating to prevent myself from going back out there. Once I had that realization, I was able to expand my life a little more. I finished a degree and started a career as opposed to just having jobs.

When I was around seven years sober, I began a two-year battle with depression. It surprised me at first, because everything was going fairly well. I had a lot of tools. I was working the Steps. I had struggled with depression off and on since I was really young. A.A. definitely helped me keep my head above water and function during that time, but I finally had to admit that I needed more than A.A. My depression was caused by a biochemical imbalance, not poor coping skills. I had to get over my false pride and a belief that my A.A. program could do it all. I finally agreed to try Prozac. What a difference it made. I hadn't realized how much I had been fighting for years to keep my depression at bay. Life got so much easier without having that battle.

Most people in A.A. have very hard times during their sobriety, and I think a solid foundation in A.A. gets you through. I'm so glad I had that solid foundation to get me through those two horrible years and lots of other not-so-bad times.

The last several years have been great. Getting married; opening up to that relationship. Being happy in my work. I'm really happy in my life. I feel good inside. I feel good in my life. Now I know I need to work with my depression when it comes back. I look at what I'm doing. I pray about it. I write. I use my tools. I call my sponsor. I call other A.A. friends. It's amazing. To me, prayer has gotten me through everything. Other tools I use a lot? My Higher Power, my spirituality, A.A. for support. Developing a network of close people I can talk to, picking up the phone.

I was recently at a meeting where this woman said to me, "Oh, I'm so glad there's someone as crazy as me." I haven't thought of myself as crazy in a long time. I don't want to be seen as having all these crazy emotions and be excused for them because I'm an alcoholic. I don't think recovery is about not doing drugs, not drinking, but still being crazy. I don't want to live like that. Crazy is not fun. Crazy is too much work. It takes too much time and effort to make amends and clean up afterwards. Drama is not attractive, either.

I've had stable relationships for almost fifteen years. I like showing up when I'm supposed to. I've been growing up to be the person I've wanted to be. Early in recovery, I didn't have good coping skills, like anger management. But I've had enough years under my belt to practice. I've found the more I behave well, the more practice I've gotten, the easier it is to do. I feel a sense of solidity within myself. I have a solid relationship with my Higher Power. People think highly of me even when they've known me for years.

Since I've been married, I've had the pleasure of seeing a whole new level of character defects. They hadn't come up before, because I wasn't challenging my intimacy skills. My husband has been very understanding. He's a great guy. He understands where I came from.

Both my parents have died. My father died when I was five years sober. Our relationship had gotten better. When I was two years sober, he gave me something that was very important to him because he was so proud of me. It really touched me. He was still a very difficult guy to get along with, so I knew we weren't ever going to have a close relationship, but it was better. At least I have some good things I can remember.

My mother and I had a very tricky relationship. She was a wonderful woman in some ways, but there was something with her low self-esteem. It was like she needed to keep me dependent on her so she could take care of me. By doing that and bailing me out all the time, I didn't have to grow. Our relationship changed when she got ill, and I finally had to help her. We got close to each other. But you know, in a funny way, when she died, I had this feeling like it was time for her to leave my life. I don't mean that in a mean way. I think of it in a spiritual sense. I couldn't have really grown up until she left. And she did. And I have grown up.

I think now that they're both gone, I have a much better understanding of my family, what did work. It's helped me to get ready, now that I'm pregnant, to create a new family and do things differently. It's been a lot of work. I've done a lot of therapy, always with people who know a lot about A.A.

You know, we come into A.A. and think, "Oh, I'll work the Steps and everything will be great," but it's more of a process. You don't do the Twelve Steps and graduate. I've done the Steps over and over and learned more about myself each time. My husband is able to point things out to me, and I'm very willing to work on myself. I like learning and growing healthier.

Early on in recovery, they told me to stick with the winners. I consciously began picking people to hang out with who were stable, who were working the Steps, who had lives I could aspire to, who had lives that were working. I didn't want to be them, but I did want some of what they had. And son-of-a-gun, it's fifteen years later and they're still sober and their lives still work, and so does mine.

CHAPTER TWELVE

Summary and Conclusions

In this chapter we will first examine the journey of recovery and some of the terms and concepts commonly used. Then we'll tie what we know about marijuana and recovery to people's stories and look for common threads among the stories to provide a complete and realistic picture of marijuana use.

Summary

When a person white-knuckles it by simply not using any drugs without any outside support, we refer to that person as being "dry" rather than "clean and sober." The difference is that a dry person still has all the emotional and behavioral habits of an active addict, whereas a clean and sober person is involved in a recovery program, and learning new ways to deal with life, including new ways of responding and behaving.

An alcoholic who isn't drinking is called "a dry drunk." Often a dry addict will say, "Well, I don't feel so much better. Life hasn't changed that much. Why go through all this effort to not use if things aren't getting much better?" When a chemically dependent person has a recovery program and learns to live life differently, however, things do get better.

The first few months of recovery are often referred to as being on a "pink cloud" of recovery, where life feels just grand! When a person in early recovery drops off that pink cloud and life starts dishing out stuff that tests his or her sobriety, then the "work" of recovery truly begins. Sometimes the drop is sudden, due to an unexpected crisis. Sometimes it's the holidays coming up for the first time and bringing with them old memories of partying or family problems they may have to face for the first time clean and sober. Sometimes the shift is gradual, almost imperceptible, with people finding they don't feel quite as good, quite as on top of things as they did for awhile. These are formidable hurdles to overcome. With support, people get through them. They sometimes miss the first few months of pink cloud recovery, but if they stay clean and sober over time, that initial "high" from the pink cloud will be replaced by a lower keyed sense of serenity that comes and goes, staying for various lengths of time.

As a chemical dependency therapist, I've seen that people have the highest likelihood of getting and remaining clean and sober if they go to Twelve Step meetings. The vast majority of treatment programs use the Twelve Step program of Alcoholics Anonymous as their central focus. When I began working in the field, I would see clients regardless of whether or not they went to Twelve Step meetings. But as I saw too many people relapse, I decided that this disease was too powerful and they needed the help of a Twelve Step program.

At the time I was going through graduate school, professors trained us to look at the underlying psychological reasons why a person drank too much or used too many drugs. In reality, most addicts would be dead if you continued to look at the so-called underlying psychological reasons. Over time, chemical dependency specialists realized that people who have progressed in their use and become chemically dependent did not do so because of some underlying psychological factors, they did so because they had a disease.

The American Medical Association now acknowledges that chemical dependency is a physical disease. It is also referred to as the addictive disease, alcoholism, or drug addiction. Psychological issues and emotional traumas may exacerbate people's use along the way, but they don't cause the disease. We also know that you can't deal effectively with those psychological problems and emotional traumas until the person is clean and sober for a while. If you delve into their emotionally charged areas too quickly, they won't have the skills or tools to deal with their emotional pain, and they'll do what they've always done; they'll numb or deaden the pain with drugs again. In other words, they'll relapse.

When working with newly sober people, counselors are often performing a kind of juggling act. They must teach their clients about their disease and let them mourn the fact that they have a chronic, relapsable, progressive, and sometimes fatal disease. Then clients must learn about and incorporate the tools of recovery into their lives. Still later, they must deal with old emotional baggage so they can live without using drugs. In the early stages of a client's recovery, I find myself being a mixture of a salesperson (selling the idea of recovery), an educator, a cheerleader, a director, and a therapist.

The term dual diagnosis is used to refer to people who have drug problems as well as major mental health problems. I often tell people who are worried about whether they're clinically depressed or have other emotional problems, "Let's see what you're like clean and sober for a while before we refer you for further psychological evaluations to see what else may be cooking." I've heard of some very unhealthy behavior that people exhibited when they were actively addicted. Most of the craziness is cleared out on its own during recovery, which surprises many people. Sometimes, however, the opposite happens and, without drugs, people fall apart emotionally (decompensate). I have also seen that happen.

I require my clients to attend Twelve Step meetings. I'll give them about six weeks to get ready and help them overcome any blocks they have about going. If they're hesitant I'll tell them, "You don't have to like it at first. It doesn't even have to make sense to you. I'll help you understand what you're hearing in meetings. But you do have to go if you want to continue working with me." Frankly, so many people relapse without the program that I'm not willing to watch them go down the tubes; it's too painful to see. Plus, I don't have the time to go to enough Al-Anon meetings to sufficiently detach from that process.

Most people who seek help for a drug problem will be out using again within a year. I assume, however, that everyone sitting in my office can and will stay clean and sober if they go to meetings, don't use in between, and work on the problems they haven't been facing for years. Many of the people I interviewed mentioned going to more meetings when they felt a need for extra support or when they were facing something big in their life.

Let's look at the people and their stories:

Debbie

Debbie is a twenty-two-year-old woman who had been using pot as her drug of choice for almost ten years when she got clean and sober through Narcotics Anonymous (N.A.). While interviewing her I was struck with her energy, her enthusiasm, her excitement. It was difficult to imagine her a few years earlier as a punk rocker with a green mohawk, or less than a year ago sitting at home, unable to work, and smoking pot all day. Her early independence and even earlier sense that something at home was wrong instilled a deep sense of knowing that she was different and didn't fit into the normal social scene at school. I was impressed with her resourcefulness and her ability to get out of difficult situations; for example, homeschooling herself so that she didn't have to deal with the school scene.

Debbie is in awe at the changes in her life in just nine short months. The fact that she has been chosen to be in management training at work is nothing short of a miracle. As I sat and interviewed Debbie in her home, the phone rang at least four times. The calls were from new friends she's met in the program since being clean and sober, all wanting to spend time with her. In fact, after we were finished at 9:30 p.m., she was going to a friend's house and they were going to go dancing at a club in town. Yes, you can have fun as a young person being clean and sober.

When she answered the phone, I noticed that her voice shifted from the heaviness of telling her life story to a lighter, easier tone with her friends. Debbie told each caller that she was being interviewed for a book about pot addiction. She was thrilled to be sharing her story and said a few times, "I hope someone reads this and gets something out of it."

Her memories of her adolescent years have not quite returned, and she's foggy on details, needing to search hard for her own personal history. I think some of that will be more clear over time. Her time perspective seemed distorted. For instance, when she talked about separating and getting back together with her husband and what happened in the few years after her parents separated I was confused, thinking she meant things lasted for longer than they had. Is this a factor of her age or has pot affected her sense of time?

Her enthusiasm and her energy level indicated to me that she was on a fast-moving "pink cloud" in recovery. Debbie's life is so full of meetings, work, friends, and social activities that it seemed almost frenzied to me, but that is not atypical. Often, newly sober people adopt one of two extreme patterns, either isolation or overstimulation. (Long-term recovery works best when a person's life is more balanced. Either extreme in the long run often leads to relapse.) At the time of our interview, Debbie was like a sponge, enthusiastically soaking up what people in the program were telling her. Over time, she'll probably find herself slowing down, meditating more, and seeing what all this really means to her. She will probably take the time to incorporate it into her life on a deeper level. But right now, she's doing what it takes to stay clean and sober one day at a time in early recovery. More insights, peace, and serenity will come with time.

Jeremy

Jeremy has been clean and sober almost a year this time. (Earlier, he had had two years and almost three months, but then used pot once.) Jeremy has an interesting story, in that he goes to meetings but not very frequently, and he hasn't quite gotten into the spiritual aspect of recovery. Look at the difference between his enthusiasm and the enthusiasm of others who have spent more time applying what they learn in meetings. Also, his responses were very concrete rather than insightful or analytical. Perhaps he's still not very comfortable with feelings and internal examination.

He hasn't incorporated the tools of the program into his life. He talks about being a little nervous because he's only done Steps One through Six. He has good reason to be nervous. At meetings you hear about a lot of people who don't work the Steps going out and relapsing. He's also still very young. He was eighteen when I talked to him, and had already had almost three years of drug-free living, so he's doing something right!

Jeremy, on the positive side, is happy and more confident about himself. I think he learned a lot from his short relapse, but still has quite a way to go. For instance, he talks about being so close to his parents, yet he never told them he relapsed. Is he afraid they'll be disappointed? Angry? Fearful? By not telling them, he is again putting on that false front that everything is okay, which he used to do in his old using days. On the other hand, everything is currently okay; he's not using and he's going to meetings occasionally.

Actually, Jeremy talks about not knowing much about his Higher Power. Well, the fact that he's spent most of the last three years clean and sober is pretty good evidence that there is a Higher Power working in his life. Considering how much a part of his life pot was, how difficult it was to be one of the only sober students in his high school, if he could spend the last three-plus years clean and sober except for one pot relapse, that should be proof enough that he could probably rely more on his Higher Power and improve the quality of his life. I just hope he allows himself the additional gifts and tools a full recovery program can offer.

Howard

We meet Howard two weeks after his first birthday of being clean and sober. Here is another person who very clearly stated he always felt like an outsider until he started smoking pot. He is enthusiastic and glad to be clean and sober, but his thoughts are still a little fuzzy and unclear. For instance, he doesn't seem very clear about the connections between his smoking marijuana and the "wreckage of his past" (an expression used in recovery to refer to the negative consequences of poor judgment and clouded thoughts).

It seems to take years of being clean and sober for the brain to clear fully from marijuana and for memories to continue coming in. Perhaps it takes a few years for the brain's synapses to clear out so recovering persons can make logical connections and see things more clearly. Howard doesn't have a lot of insights into the extent of impairment he experienced by smoking pot chronically for so many years, but you wouldn't expect a marijuana addict with only one year clean and sober to be able to see clearly yet. He hasn't looked at what it meant that he smoked an illegal substance for twenty-five years and justified that on a daily basis as he worked in the legal profession. He hasn't seen how pot distorted his judgment, possibly leading to his business failures. There were some facts about pot he didn't know which surprised me—that pot stays in your system for about one year, or that the pot he was smoking at the end of his career was at least 200 times stronger than what he had been smoking when he started.

Howard has a strong link with his A.A. program, yet still has drug hunger crop up when he wonders, "Would what I'm doing right now be enhanced with pot?" If Howard can incorporate Step One—that life is unmanageable and we are powerless over this disease—he'll be okay. He needs to

167

stay close to the program, his sponsor, and his Higher Power. At least he is conscious of the disease talking, while others are not. He's also serious about wanting more of what he's gotten in the last few years working various recovery programs. Those two factors are definitely in his favor.

Like Debbie, Howard had a kind of fast-paced feel about him. As a drug therapist I've found that when clients had used within twenty-four hours of coming to my office, they were very fast paced—their breathing, even their talking was fast-paced, clipped, pointed, or sharp in its tone. With Debbie and Howard, I experienced a somewhat similar, but less extreme response from their energy. I've experienced that before with people who are on a fast-paced "pink cloud" of recovery. They're busy, on some level, convincing themselves this lifestyle (being drug free) is really great. They need that enthusiasm to keep going, to keep trying new drug-free behavior that may feel uncomfortable at first. Their zest is useful in a funny kind of way. Remember, it is much easier for an addict to continue using drugs than to stop using drugs.

Over time, recovering addicts almost magically begin experiencing moments, then minutes, then hours, then days, then weeks, and then even months of serenity. It's one of the "gifts" of A.A. when you follow the suggestions outlined in the Twelve Steps of recovery.

Josh

Josh is a young man whose minority background has caused him a great deal of shame and discomfort. He couldn't change his cultural heritage, and he never felt like he fit in. From the first time he smoked pot, he had a sense of belonging, of having arrived, of his dream coming true.

That lasted two years, and then his life became a nightmare until he entered a rehab center.

I think it's clear as you read Josh's story how different his life is from Debbie's and Howard's. He has a good few years in the program. He feels more settled in his life. He's happy with what he's doing. He's grateful to the program for providing him guidelines that he can use on a daily basis. He's incorporated elements of the A.A. program into his life. He gave a lot of service at meetings the first years, and is now transferring the A.A. idea of giving away what you've been given, to tutoring other students. I think that's the difference between "talking the talk," and "walking the walk" or "living the life" of a recovering person. In order to stay clean and sober over time, and not relapse, you have to live differently on a daily basis.

Josh needs to remember that just because a recovering person hasn't used drugs for a period of time doesn't mean he or she is cured. Addiction (including marijuana addiction) is a chronic, progressive, relapsable, and sometimes fatal disease. Many people with twenty-plus years of sobriety say things like, "Every day I try and remember to be grateful for another day's reprieve from using and ask for the willingness not to use today." The keys to staying sober seem to be admitting you are powerless over all mind-altering drugs, having a strong relationship with a power greater than yourself, honesty in all your affairs, being able to ask for help when you need it, and remaining humble. In my practice, I have seen people have the most success who have incorporated these elements into their lives. People who experience years of drug-free living and serenity have learned how to use the steps of A.A. in all aspects of their lives. I wish this success for Josh.

Dan

Dan's interview seemed to be on a more cerebral level than most other people's. He is very clear as to how the A.A. program and recovery have enhanced his life. He's still somewhat in awe of his own denial for years and the power that marijuana had over his judgment and his life. Dan repeated on three different occasions how subtle marijuana is and how much it impairs your life, yet you don't realize it until after you've stopped smoking for a few years. This was an important point that he wanted to share with others. He also expressed a good deal of anger at marijuana advocates who are not presenting an accurate picture of marijuana.

The other issue that came up repeatedly in Dan's story was the importance of the work ethic he picked up from his mother and her family. The message wasn't just "work," and not just "work hard," but "work very hard to prove yourself." It's no wonder Dan's such a successful physician in his field. He is highly respected and has definitely "proven" himself, but at what price?

Dan took the same kinds of risks as Howard. Both were jeopardizing their entire professional career each time they lit up a joint or smoked a pipeful. Both expressed that smoking marijuana was just what you did back then, only they extended "back then" into their adult professional life. That is the power of denial! That is the power of marijuana!

Dan chuckled as he recalled thinking how ludicrous people in A.A. seemed to him at first when they said they were grateful alcoholics and addicts; yet over the last six years, he has become one himself. He credits his recovery program and the support system he has developed since being in recovery with helping him through this difficult crisis with his daughter. He said, "Without this program I'd be using, but with this program, I can go one day at a time, remembering

God doesn't give us more than we can handle. I've cried at a couple of meetings, my boundaries aren't so clear right now, but I'm not using and I'm staying close to my program." He knows how to get help for himself.

Dan said that when he entered recovery he needed to very clearly change hats and not be an expert as he was in his work. In fact, he said it was a relief to not have to be the expert and just be "Dan the addict" who needed help. If he had not been able to make that switch, he'd most probably be back out using marijuana again.

Grant

I had known Grant professionally but never knew details about his personal history until he agreed to be interviewed for this book. I listened as he recalled in vivid detail the many years he spent being high. I felt upset as I realized how many productive years he had lost, how he had lost his children, his untapped talent, and his historical justifications for those losses. Although Grant has been drug free for over ten years, he doesn't consider himself to have been free of toxic thoughts until he began going to A.A. meetings six years ago.

Finally at one point late in the interview I said, "Grant, if you don't mind me saying so, it seems to me that you're still minimizing the role pot played in your life and the consequences you suffered." "In what ways?" he questioned me. "Well, as a therapist, what I see is that you pretty much 'lost' at least eight years out of your life and you lost your family. In fact, you lost your family in two ways: (A) your wife left and took the children clear across the country so you were hardly ever able to see them, and (B) during the few years when you did live with them you were too stoned to really be there and notice or take part in their lives."

At first Grant repeated that he thought Cynthia left because he had begun smoking cigarettes again. "Oh come on," I spontaneously responded, "Do you really think that smoking cigarettes would break up a marriage? I would imagine that the years of craziness when you smoked all the time and were barely functional from smoking grass were probably more important."

"Wow," he said, "I'll have to think about that. I never saw it like that before. Isn't it incredible, even after this much time, I can still not have a clear picture? Thank you, I'll get back to you about this." About a week later we talked and he thanked me for my insights and said something like, "Boy, does that just prove my point about the insidious nature of this drug. I honestly hadn't seen grass as being that big a deal. I saw more "bottoms" with alcohol. But pot was a major factor in a lot of crazy and painful situations. You were right about the lost years and my family. I'm going to need to work on that some more. I love these insights that keep coming. They take time but I never would have gotten them at all if I was still stoned."

Grant's story provides many examples of how marijuana distorts reality, judgment, and decision-making abilities. Here was a smart man who had read lots of science books as a child, who had science experiments going on for years. He grew up thinking in a linear, scientific fashion naturally, yet after he started smoking pot, all those natural talents and curiosities went by the wayside. He dropped his early interests and ways of examining the world. In hindsight, some of his decisions look very questionable. He was operating from a strong commitment to make our world very different and believed in what he was doing at the time. Would he have made the same decisions if he hadn't been high so much of the time?

Let's look at some examples of his distorted thinking while he was using marijuana regularly. Grant emigrated to Europe with his family soon after he finished graduate school because he was sure this country was about to break out in a full scale civil war along age lines. How realistic was that assessment? Earlier, when he and Cynthia were about to break up but failed to raise money for an abortion, they took the meager amount of money they had gathered, went to Mexico, and got married! It seemed okay for Cynthia to smoke pot all through her pregnancy. Unfortunately, their son has had to live with the consequences. And what about all those years when Grant was part of the West Coast commune scene that he described as "magical years?" What's so magical about losing your family, being loaded all the time, and being so out of touch with reality that you think you're part of a big change in the world that isn't actually happening? Still later, when he moved to Santa Cruz and was working for the "nurturing" grassroots organization but not producing anything, he never saw himself as ripping off the system. He wasn't frustrated by his lack of productivity. He simply appreciated the so-called creative process despite the fact that it wasn't going anywhere. And, even knowing for a couple of years that smoking pot was not good for him, that he was having anxiety attacks and heart palpitations, he still continued to smoke.

Grant and Dan both lost a parent during their growing-up years. Most teenagers feel a fair amount of emotional pain just in being who they are—there are so many pressures, so many rules of how to fit in, so many areas in which to judge yourself or be judged and see if you "measure up." The pain of losing a parent is so great that not only teenagers but adults, too, want to dull the pain or make it go away entirely. At how many funerals has the spouse been prescribed Valium to help deal with grief so he or she can sleep or even function? Teens reason, "If adults use prescription drugs or alcohol, and pot works well for me, why not pursue it?" Our cultural role models say, "You don't have to feel bad" or "Take this; it'll make you feel better." I think the timing was right for Grant and Dan. Pot was available, and it made them feel better by taking some of their pain and grief away. The pain of losing a parent was too much to handle without some outside intervention. Rather than seeing a therapist, they used marijuana.

Alicia

When I interviewed Alicia, a woman I had worked with for five years and thought I knew very well, I was amazed by some of the things she said. I hadn't seen her in three years, and during that time, she had been making more sense out of her personal and drug history. More of her memories had surfaced; thus the overall picture was more clear. After the interview, when we were both sharing our reactions, she realized that during our early work together, when we first talked about early personal history, she was so toxic and still dealing with major memory losses that she wasn't able to recall much. Other memories she didn't mention because she didn't know they were relevant. Many of the memories I heard during our interview had never come up during our therapy sessions.

Alicia was born with physical handicaps that might have been far more serious if her parents had not brought her to specialists throughout her childhood. Between her parents' determination and her own, her physical handicaps were all but overcome. Their most powerful scars were Alicia's own sense of being special, different, and "better than"— a sense definitely reinforced by her family's credo.

From almost the first time she smoked pot she had a wonderful sense of relief and belonging. She smoked pot for the next twenty years, until even an alarm watch couldn't help her keep track of things, and until she found herself on the verge of physically abusing her children. Recovery came for Alicia at just the right time, and she fought long and hard to catch up with her twenty "high" years. Her measure of serenity after seven years in the program is a wonderful example of the A.A. promises coming true.

Phil

Interviewing Phil brought back old memories and allowed me to catch up on the last five years of his life. I was able to fill him in on my perspective of his early recovery since he seems to have lost a lot of those memories. After we finished the formal interview we were able to talk.

Phil had a complex childhood, moving from the north to the south, from money to no money, from the United States to Europe. It was clear that his values, morals, and academics changed when he started smoking pot and "tripped" for the first time. It seems that he didn't find any measure of happiness in his life (except for the feeling of belonging he had in Europe with his friends) until he was in recovery. That's a long time to wait.

As I heard his story, how much he drank and got drunk when he didn't like the taste, the high, or his subsequent behavior, I was again struck with how powerful this disease is. He lived such an emotionally painful life for at least ten years, crying himself through the weekends. Yet he was completely out of touch with what was causing his pain, the substances he depended on to "keep his balance"— marijuana, alcohol, and sometimes cocaine.

His story is also an excellent example of how hard someone has to work to come back from this disease. I know he's worked hard, yet he's still battling some of the same issues he was five years ago—a tendency to "go away" with his work, an inability to relax in the evenings, continued difficulty believing he's worthy of special things he can now afford.

It was wonderful to hear how much he's enjoying being a father. It's gratifying to hear he is able to give his son what he wants and needs. And just as he's helping his son to grow, his son is also bringing him joy and helping him continue to grow. He isn't repeating his family's pattern of being emotionally unavailable.

When people work as hard as he has worked and continually fail to make significant progress in areas they'd like to change, they are often clinically depressed. That means they have a second biochemically based disease—depression. Medication can help tremendously. I suggested he talk to his therapist about depression. He said his therapist had suggested it a couple of times, but he had thought, "I'm an addict; I shouldn't take that stuff; I'm afraid I'll get addicted." The antidepressant drugs being used today are not addictive. They also are not like the old "happy pills" (uppers) of past years. They simply balance the brain chemistry so the person is not walking around under a black cloud or feeling as if he or she has extra weights around the ankles. They seem to free up a person's psychic energy to make the changes he or she wants to make. Often a person only has to take an antidepressant for six months or so; then once the brain chemistry is balanced, he or she can live comfortably without medication.

Margie

Margie had twelve years of sobriety when she was interviewed for this book. She seemed enthusiastic and truly grateful for the changes in her life. I was struck with how she viewed her time in recovery as a "miracle" and a "gift," rather than being proud of it. After the interview, when we were talking informally, she said, "I haven't done anything I'm ashamed of in years. I'm never afraid when someone calls my name out loudly. I always used to cringe and worry that I had done something wrong. It's so nice this way!"

Margie had an interesting perspective about her past. She doesn't miss those days and doesn't dwell on them. She didn't really want to talk about specific people or things because, as she said, "I'm past the blaming stage. I know I made some lousy choices, like, in the relationship department, but I see them as lousy choices, whereas I used to blame the 'jerks' who 'screwed me over.' Yeah, I went with some jerks, but most of them had the same problem as I did, only I chose men who used more than I, so I didn't look so bad. Why rag on them now? That's old and done. That was my old life. What's happening today is more important."

Margie seems to be living the A.A. philosophy of "one day at a time" in the present tense rather than dwelling on the past or worrying about the future. When I commented that it looked that way to me, she responded with characteristic honesty, "It's much more like that, but some days are better than others. We strive for progress, not perfection in this program." She seems to have a spontaneous, spirited, enthusiastic, and energetic style. She said she was still hoping for "longer moments of serenity to invade."

She had clearly benefited greatly from being in A.A. and had allowed herself to use antidepressant medication when

177

she realized that her own natural coping skills were not a match for her years of physical and emotional hardships. She didn't go into detail, but one knew she had truly suffered from pain, loss, and not being able to solve it with tools she was so used to relying upon. She had "swallowed her pride" and relied on Western medicine. It had allowed her to move forward and "inhabit her own body again."

Jillian

Jillian has the longest time in sobriety. She had truly "given herself over to A.A." for many years. It had changed her life. I was struck during the interview with how many times she had realized alcohol was a problem, tried to stop drinking unsuccessfully and then gone back into the painful, full-blown, partying lifestyle. She reiterated how she never saw marijuana as a drug or a problem; it was just something she did every day—eat, sleep, and smoke. She struggled with paranoia for at least three years before giving up the marijuana, and has never been paranoid since. If her denial about marijuana isn't indicative of marijuana's powerful ability to affect a person's perceptions, judgments, and decisions, what is? Just look at how different her life is from what it was. At one point she said, "You know, if I looked at my life today back then, I would look at it with disdain. Really, back then I would have only had disparaging comments to make. But I love my life now." Being in recovery has allowed Jillian to become who she had always wanted to be and not who she was stuck being.

It took Jillian a long time to accept her depression as a second chemical imbalance which she could not control or cure. It is interesting that both Margie and Jillian were willing to try antidepressants only after many years of sobriety and after realizing they were as powerless over their depression as they had been over their addictions. When they accepted depression as an illness in their lives they knew they had not caused it, could not control it, nor could they cure it. They both said it had been a difficult "pride thing" for them to overcome, but both expressed appreciation and gratitude for the help they have received from their prescribed medication. They felt they could once again use their tools of recovery to deal effectively with "regular old" life issues that came along.

Reality changes over time when you're in recovery. The way you look at your current everyday life experiences changes when you are no longer conning yourself or others that everything is "fine" when it's not. And your personal history changes as more memories flood in. When you no longer have your drug-induced reality to defend anymore, you can remember things that contradicted how you had wanted to see yourself, things that you couldn't allow before. That can be very exciting, scary, freeing, embarrassing, and frightening stuff. The Twelve Steps of recovery, meetings, a good sponsor, and a skilled therapist with a strong knowledge of chemical dependency can be very helpful as these discrepancies emerge.

Conclusions

It is certainly clear from these people's stories, which range in time from nine months clean and sober to fifteen years, that life can change drastically in sobriety. People who lived their whole lives feeling like they didn't fit in anywhere without marijuana can grow up in sobriety fitting into their own bodies and selves. They can feel taken care of by a higher power, and can develop a healthy support system in their recovery program and with other people in their lives, even those who are not in the program.

It is also clear that pot is not a harmless drug to be used with no consequences. Besides the fact that it is illegal and could send a person to jail, it can can also cause someone to lose years out of his or her life and experience years of mental and emotional pain. As Alicia so aptly put it in her story, "Trying to play catch-up is not easy." But all people agreed it was definitely worth the effort. The difference in how people felt at the end of their "using" days and how they felt when they were interviewed is remarkable. One person said, "It just keeps getting better." And many people have said, "My worst days in recovery have never been as bad as my last days being high."

The original *fun* involved in smoking marijuana and being *high* disappeared before these people found themselves in recovery. They looked for it; they searched hard every day, but couldn't find it. When all else had failed, they turned to recovery, realizing they had a big problem. With varying degrees of hope and faith, they plodded through until they felt better and life became joyful again.

The keys to staying sober seem to be: (1) admitting you are powerless over all mind-altering drugs; (2) having a strong relationship with a power greater than youself; (3) honesty in all your affairs; (4) being able to ask for help when you need it; and (5) remaining humble. In my practice, I have seen people have the most success who have incorporated these elements into their lives. These are all principles of the Twelve Steps of A.A.

People who experience years of drug-free living and serenity have learned how to use the Twelve Steps of A.A. in all aspects of their lives. They do not necessarily go to many meetings a week; instead, they take the information they've learned and they "practice the principles (of A.A.) in all their affairs."

180

Do You Have a Problem with Marijuana?

If you're wondering whether you may have a problem with marijuana, or if you're wondering whether someone else in your life may have a problem, ask yourself three important questions:

1. Is there a loss of control when I start smoking? (In other words, do you say you'll only smoke a couple of hits and then end up really stoned? Or do you think you're only going to have a beer and then find yourself smoking pot, too?)

2. Is there a compulsion to use? (Do you find yourself saying, "I can't wait till my day is done and I can fire up a joint?")

3. Do I continue to use in the face of negative effects? (Is your family upset with you? Do you get into lots of arguments? Do you find yourself increasingly irritable with people? Are you intolerant of people who don't use, sure you're cool and they aren't? Have you lost a job or feel your job performance isn't what it could be? Do you tend to miss appointments or forget about responsibilities on Mondays? Do you feel paranoid?)

If you've answered "Yes" to these questions, then you probably have a problem. For even more evidence of your possible dependence on Marijuana, see the questionnaire from Marijuana Anonymous in the Appendix. It is my hope that after you've read this book, you won't feel quite as scared to deal with your drug problems as you did before. Find yourself a good drug counselor and some meetings. Call Marijuana Anonymous or try Alcoholics Anonymous, and watch your life change.

Appendix

References

Alcoholics Anonymous. *Big Book.* Alcoholics Anonymous World Services, Inc., 1955.

Bower, Bruce. "'Day After' Effects of Pot Smoking." *Science News* (November 16, 1985), p. 310.

Cohn, Jordan E. "The Perils of Pot." *Seventeen.* May 1986, pp. 156–157.

Flynn, Ramsey, and Steven D. Kaye. "Collision at Gunpow." *Reader's Digest.* May 1988, pp. 120–127.

Gallagher, Winifred. "Marijuana: Is There New Reason to Worry?" *American Health.* March 1988, pp. 92–94.

Gold, Mark, S. *Marijuana.* New York: Plenum Publishing Corporation, 1989.

Guttman, Monica. "The New Pot Culture." *Denver Post,* February 18, 1996, pp. 4–7.

Gwynne, Peter. "Marijuana." *Glamour.* October 1984, p. 154.

Hymes, Donna. "Marijuana Update: New Reasons to 'Keep Off the Grass.'" *Current Health 2.* March 1987, pp. 18–21.

Malone, Joan. "Marijuana Makes a Comeback." *Mademoiselle.* October 1990, pp. 184–187.

"Marijuana and Pilot's Performance." *USA Today.* Vol. 115. August 1986, p. 13.

"Marijuana Use May Cause Mental Problems." *Jet.* September 28, 1987, p. 28.

McCarthy, Paul. "Pot Peril." *American Health.* December 1989, p. 16.

Meer, Jeff. "Marijuana in the Air: Delayed Buzz Bomb." [research by Jerome Yesavage and Von Otto Leier] *Psychology Today,* Vol. 20, February 1986, p. 68.

Oliwenstein, Lori. "The Perils of Pot." *Discover.* June 1988, p. 18.

Porterfield, Kay Marie. "Marijuana and Learning: Grass gets an F." *Current Health 2.* January 1989, pp. 20–27.

Richard, Jerome. "Pot Buster." *American Health.* June 1991, p. 14.

Schwartz, Richard, H. "Marijuana Mangles Memory." *Science News.* November 18, 1989, p. 332.

Sherman, Carl. "Marijuana Report: the Latest Dope on Its Dangers." *Mademoiselle.* June 1985, p. 48.

Siegel, B.Z., Lindley Garnier, and S.M. Siegel. "Mercury in Marijuana." *BioScience.* October 1988, pp. 619–623.

Steele, William. "The Downside of Smoking Tobacco and Marijuana." *Current Health 2.* November 1989, pp. 24–26.

Wood, Virchel E. "Drug Abuse Tragedies Observed by Orthopedic Surgeon." Loma Linda University, School of Medicine, Department of Orthopedic Surgery, 1994.

Information About
Alcoholics Anonymous (A.A.)

General Service Office
P.O. Box 459
Grand Central Station
New York, NY 10163
(212) 870-3400
Fax #: (212) 870-3003
TTY#: (212) 870-3199

Alcoholics Anonymous (A.A.) is a fellowship of men and women who share their experience, strength, and hope with each other that they may solve their common problem and help others to recover from alcoholism.

The only requirement for membership is a desire to stop drinking. There are no fees for A.A. membership; we are self-supporting through our own contributions. A.A. is not allied with any sect, denomination, politics, organization or institution; does not wish to engage in any controversy; neither endorses nor opposes any causes. Our primary purpose is to stay sober and help other alcoholics to achieve sobriety.

The Twelve Steps and Twelve Traditions are reprinted with permission of Alcoholics Anonymous World Services, Inc. Permission to reprint and adapt the Twelve Steps and Twelve Traditions does not mean that A.A. has reviewed or approved the contents of this publication, nor that A.A. Agrees with the views expressed herein. A.A. is a program of recovery from alcoholism only—use of the Steps and Traditions in connection with programs and activities which are patterned after A.A., but which address other problems, or in any other non-A.A. context, does not imply otherwise.

The Twelve Steps of Alcoholics Anonymous (A.A.)

1. We admitted we were powerless over alcohol—that our lives had become unmanageable.
2. Came to believe that a Power greater than ourselves could restore us to sanity.
3. Made a decision to turn our will and our lives over to the care of God as we understood Him.
4. Made a searching and fearless moral inventory of ourselves.
5. Admitted to God, to ourselves, and to another human being the exact nature of our wrongs.
6. Were entirely ready to have God remove all these defects of character.
7. Humbly asked Him to remove our shortcomings.
8. Made a list of all persons we had harmed, and became willing to make amends to them all.
9. Made direct amends to such people wherever possible, except when to do so would injure them or others.
10. Continued to take personal inventory and when we were wrong promptly admitted it.
11. Sought through prayer and meditation to improve our conscious contact with God, as we understood Him, praying only for knowledge of His will for us and the power to carry that out.
12. Having had a spiritual awakening as the result of these steps, we tried to carry this message to alcoholics, and to practice these principles in all our affairs.

The Twelve Traditions of
Alcoholics Anonymous (A.A.)

1. Our common welfare should come first; personal recovery depends upon A.A. unity.

2. For our group purpose, there is but one ultimate authority—a loving God as He may express Himself in our group conscience. Our leaders are but trusted servants; they do not govern.

3. The only requirement for A.A. membership is a desire to stop drinking.

4. Each group should be autonomous except in matters affecting other groups or A.A. as a whole.

5. Each group has but one primary purpose—to carry its message to the alcoholic who still suffers.

6. An A.A. group ought never endorse, finance, lend the A.A. name to any related facility or outside enterprise, lest problems of money, property, and prestige divert us from our primary purpose.

7. Every A.A. group ought to be fully self-supporting, declining outside contributions.

8. Alcoholics Anonymous should remain forever non-professional, but our service centers may employ special workers.

9. A.A., as such, ought never be organized; but we may create service boards or committees directly responsible to those they serve.

10. Alcoholics Anonymous has no opinion on outside issues; hence the A.A. name ought never be drawn into public controversy.

11. Our public relations policy is based on attraction rather than promotion; we need always maintain personal anonymity at the level of press, radio, and films.

12. Anonymity is the spiritual foundation of all our traditions, ever reminding us to place principles before personalities.

Information About
Marijuana Anonymous (M.A.)

Marijuana Anonymous World Services
P.O. Box 2912
Van Nuys, CA 91404
1-800-766-6779

How It Works

The practice of rigorous honesty, of opening our hearts and minds, and the willingness to go to any lengths to have a spiritual awakening are essential to our recovery.

Our old ideas and ways of life no longer work for us. Our suffering shows us that we need to let go absolutely. We surrender ourselves to a Power greater than ourselves.

Do not be discouraged; none of us are saints. Our program is not easy, but it is simple. We strive for progress not perfection. Our experiences before and after we entered recovery teach us three important ideas:

• that we are marijuana addicts and cannot manage our own lives;

• that probably no human power can relieve our addiction; and

• that our Higher Power can and will if sought.

The Twelve Steps and Twelve Traditions are reprinted with permission of Marijuana Anonymous World Services, Inc. Permission to reprint the Twelve Steps and Twelve Traditions does not imply that M.A. is in any way affiliated with this book or its author(s). (Although the Twelve Steps of M.A. are patterned after the Twelve Steps of Alcoholics Anonymous, with permission, the two programs are not affiliated.)

The Twelve Steps of Marijuana Anonymous (M.A.)

1. We admitted we were powerless over marijuana, that our lives had become unmanageable.
2. Came to believe that a Power greater than ourselves could restore us to sanity.
3. Made a decision to turn our will and our lives over to the care of God, *as we understood God.*
4. Made a searching and fearless moral inventory of ourselves.
5. Admitted to God, to ourselves, and to another human being the exact nature of our wrongs.
6. Were entirely ready to have God remove all these defects of character.
7. Humbly asked God to remove our shortcomings.
8. Made a list of all persons we had harmed, and became willing to make amends to them all.
9. Made direct amends to such people wherever possible, except when to do so would injure them or others.
10. Continued to take personal inventory and when we were wrong, promptly admitted it.
11. Sought through prayer and meditation to improve out conscious contact with God, *as we understood God,* praying only for knowledge of God's will for us and the power to carry that out.
12. Having had a spiritual awakening as the result of these steps, we tried to carry this message to marijuana addicts and to practice these principles in all our affairs.

The Twelve Traditions of Marijuana Anonymous (M.A.)

1. Our common welfare should come first; personal recovery depends on M.A. unity.
2. For our group purpose there is but one ultimate authority, a loving God whose expression may come through in our group conscience. Our leaders are but trusted servants; they do not govern.
3. The only requirement for membership is a desire to stop using marijuana.
4. Each group should be autonomous except in matters affecting other groups or M.A. as a whole.
5. Each group has but one primary purpose, to carry its message to the marijuana addict who still suffers.
6. M.A. groups ought never endorse, finance, or lend the M.A. name to any related facility or outside enterprise, lest problems of money, property, and prestige divert us from our primary purpose.
7. M.A. groups ought to be fully self-supporting, declining outside contributions.
8. Marijuana Anonymous (M.A.) should remain forever nonprofessional, but our service centers may employ special workers.
9. M.A., as such, ought never be organized, but we may create service boards or committees directly responsible to those they serve.
10. Marijuana Anonymous has no opinion on outside issues; hence the M.A. name ought never to be drawn into public controversy.
11. Our public relations policy is based upon attraction rather than promotion; we need always maintain personal anonymity at the level of press, radio, TV, film, and other public media. We need guard with special care the anonymity of all fellow M.A. members.
12. Anonymity is the spiritual foundation of all our traditions, ever reminding us to place principles before personalities.

Twelve Questions to Determine Whether Marijuana Is a Problem in Your Life

The following questions from Marijuana Anonymous may help you determine whether marijuana is a problem in your life. If you answer yes to any of these questions, then you may want to consider getting help.

1. Has smoking pot stopped being fun?
2. Do you ever get high alone?
3. Is it hard for you to imagine life without marijuana?
4. Do you find your friends are determined by your marijuana use?
5. Do you smoke marijuana to avoid dealing with your problems?
6. Do you smoke pot to cope with your feelings?
7. Does your marijuana use let you live in a privately defined world?
8. Have you ever failed to keep promises you made about cutting down or controlling your dope smoking?
9. Has your use of marijuana caused problems with memory, concentration, or motivation?
10. When your stash is nearly empty, do you feel anxious or worried about how to get more?
11. Do you plan your life around marijuana use?
12. Have friends or relatives ever complained that your pot smoking is damaging your relationship with them?

Organizations That Can Help

Al-Anon
Al-Anon Family Group Headquarters
1600 Corporate Landing Parkway
Virginia Beach, VA 23454-5617
804-563-1600

Alateen
1372 Broadway
New York, NY 10018-0862
212-302-7240

Alcoholics Anonymous (A.A.)
General Services Office
P.O. Box 459
Grand Central Station
New York, NY 10163
212-870-3400

Children of Alcoholics Foundation, Inc. (COAF)
P.O. Box 4185
Grand Central Station
New York, NY 10022
212-754-0656

Families Anonymous
World Services Office
P.O. Box 528
Van Nuys, CA 91408

Hazelden
15251 Pleasant Valley Road
Center City, MN 55012
800-328-9000
www.hazelden.org

Marijuana Anonymous (M.A.)
World Services Office
P.O. Box 2912
Van Nuys, CA 91404
800-766-6779

Narcotics Anonymous (N.A.)
World Service Office
P.O. Box 9999
Van Nuys, CA 91409
818-780-3951

National Association for Children of Alcoholics (NACOA)
11426 Rockville Pike, Suite 100
Rockville, MD 20852
301-468-0985

National Clearinghouse for Alcohol & Drug Information
(NCADI)
11426 Rockville Pike
Rockville, MD 20852
301-468-2600

National Council on Alcoholism and Drug Dependence
(NCADD)
12 West 21st Street
New York, NY 10010
212-206-6770